WHAT READERS

It's a clever idea—really ... the eternal joy of the resur ... onal stories from Baptism through our funerals and beyond. It's invariably the story of Christ, but we always read ourselves right in it. Dr. Filipek's style is constantly speaking directly to the reader, a very inviting way to catechize those entirely new to the faith. The Six Chief Parts and Lutheran worship (even closed Communion) are presented in their biblical contexts!

> —**Dr. Carl C. Fickenscher II,** professor of pastoral ministry and missions, Concordia Theological Seminary, Fort Wayne, Indiana; speaker and author; editor of *Concordia Pulpit Resources*

I have a friend who does drone photography. With a bird's-eye view, what you thought you knew intimately unfolds in wonder from a wider, higher perspective. Dr. Filipek's new book, *Life in Christ: Rooted, Woven, and Grafted into God's Story*, grants readers such an experience with the Sacred Scriptures. Rather than "losing the forest for the trees," this work enables readers to glimpse the grand sweep of the greatest story ever told. They'll walk away marveling at how it centers on Jesus from the beginning and connects to us right here in our own world.

> —**William Weedon,** assistant pastor, St. Paul Lutheran Church, Hamel, Illinois

With pastoral passion, Adam Filipek calls us to not abandon our first love, Christ. The reason is not found in obligation but in the delight that God deigns to dwell with us. *Life in Christ* faithfully grounds its readers in the narrative of Scripture that then flows into the ongoing life of the Church so that we might be blessed with life in Christ.

> —**Kevin Golden,** PhD; associate professor of exegetical theology, Concordia Seminary, St. Louis, Missouri

To know the entire Bible is a good thing for every Christian. Whether it is a lifelong Christian, someone new to the faith, or someone somewhere in between, they may discover that reading the Bible is challenging, especially when they want to find the connection between the stories and statements in the sixty-six books of the Bible. What helps in that situation is for the reader to be mindful of two things: First, that he looks to Christ and sees what Christ has done as central to Scripture. Second, as a reader, he does not read Scripture unaffected by Christ's ministry but rather sees himself as someone who has been grafted into the Body of Christ through Baptism, who attends a church and worships the triune God. Reading Scripture is a theocentric endeavor looking outward toward what God has done in Christ for me; it is not anthropocentric in orientation—all about me and my personal desires. The Bible is also not only an accumulation of separate stories or doctrines. To that end, the author draws the reader into Scripture from Eden to Christ's return and success-fully builds a bridge from texts to the personal life of the reader so that Scripture speaks about my creation, my redemption, and my sanctification. This is a book written for a broad audience, pastors and laity alike, and it is written in an easy, readable style.

—**Klaus Detlev Schulz**, professor of pastoral ministry and missions; dean of graduate studies; director of PhD in missiology program; and director of inter-national studies at Concordia Theological Seminary, Fort Wayne, Indiana

LIFE IN CHRIST

Rooted, Woven, and Grafted
into God's Story

ADAM T. FILIPEK

Published by Concordia Publishing House

3558 S. Jefferson Avenue, St. Louis, MO 63118-3968

1-800-325-3040 ● cph.org

Written by Adam T. Filipek

Edited by Wayne Palmer

Figures 4–9 are images of stained glass windows at Immanuel Lutheran Church in Lidgerwood, North Dakota.

Manufactured in the United States of America

1 2 3 4 5 6 7 8 9 10   32 31 30 29 28 27 26 25 24 23

Dedicated to the saints of Holy Cross Lutheran Church and Immanuel Lutheran Church in Lidgerwood, North Dakota.

For I decided to know nothing among you except Jesus Christ and Him crucified.

1 Corinthians 2:2

For you have died, and your life is hidden with Christ in God. When Christ who is your life appears, then you also will appear with Him in glory.

Colossians 3:3–4

TABLE OF CONTENTS

ACKNOWLEDGMENTS

Chiefly, I am indebted to my Lord and Savior, Jesus Christ, who has called me out of darkness into His marvelous light of salvation. Without Him, I would be lost forever. But He has delivered me from sin, death, and the devil. To Him, with the Father and the Holy Spirit, be all blessing, glory, wisdom, thanksgiving, honor, power, and might, now and ever, unto ages of ages. Amen!

Additionally, this book would not have been possible without the prayers, love, and support of the saints of Holy Cross Lutheran Church and Immanuel Lutheran Church in Lidgerwood, North Dakota. I am truly privileged, honored, and blessed to serve as their pastor, and I owe them an inexpressible debt of gratitude and thanksgiving for all they have done for me, with a special thank you to those who have participated in *Life in Christ* (adult instruction) every time that it has been offered.

Moreover, I am grateful for my brother, Rev. Aaron M. Filipek, who served as a makeshift theological consultant on numerous occasions. He was always ready and willing to listen to a paragraph or two, even if I called him at the most inopportune times, and he would tell me if my wording was theologically accurate.

Finally, a special acknowledgment and recognition is owed not only to my children, David, Miriam, Jacob, and Bethany, who sacrificed countless hours of playtime with their father, but evermore to my wife, Becky, for her unwavering assistance and encouragement. In the preparation of this manuscript, she devoted incalculable hours to copyediting and proofreading. Without her this not make sense does, but because of her I'm not missing or mincing any words. I am incessantly grateful for this amazing, God-fearing woman who the Lord has given to me.

ABBREVIATIONS

Books of the Bible

Gn . . . . Genesis	**Ezr** . . . . Ezra	**Jl** . . . . Joel
Ex . . . . Exodus	**Ne** . . . . Nehemiah	**Am** . . . . Amos
Lv . . . . Leviticus	**Est** . . . . Esther	**Ob** . . . . Obadiah
Nu . . . . Numbers	**Jb** . . . . Job	**Jnh** . . . . Jonah
Dt . . . . Deuteronomy	**Ps** . . . . Psalms	**Mi** . . . . Micah
Jsh . . . . Joshua	**Pr** . . . . Proverbs	**Na** . . . . Nahum
Jgs . . . . Judges	**Ec** . . . . Ecclesiastes	**Hab** . . . . Habakkuk
Ru . . . . Ruth	**Sg** . . . . Song of Solomon	**Zep** . . . . Zephaniah
1Sm . . . . 1 Samuel	**Is** . . . . Isaiah	**Hg** . . . . Haggai
2Sm . . . . 2 Samuel	**Jer** . . . . Jeremiah	**Zec** . . . . Zechariah
1Ki . . . . 1 Kings	**Lm** . . . . . . Lamentations	**Mal** . . . . Malachi
2Ki . . . . 2 Kings	**Ezk** . . . . Ezekiel	
1Ch . . . . 1 Chronicles	**Dn** . . . . Daniel	
2Ch . . . . 2 Chronicles	**Hos** . . . . Hosea	

Mt .... Matthew	**Eph** .... Ephesians	**Heb** .... Hebrews
Mk .... Mark	**Php** .... Philippians	**Jas** .... James
Lk .... Luke	**Col** .... Colossians	**1Pt** .... 1 Peter
Jn .... John	**1Th** .... 1 Thessalonians	**2Pt** .... 2 Peter
Ac .... Acts	**2Th** ... 2 Thessalonians	**1Jn** .... 1 John
Rm. .... Romans	**1Tm** .... 1 Timothy	**2Jn** .... 2 John
1Co .... 1 Corinthians	**2Tm** .... 2 Timothy	**3Jn** .... 3 John
2Co ...... 2 Corinthians	**Ti** .... Titus	**Jude** .... Jude
Gal .... Galatians	**Phm** .... Philemon	**Rv** .... Revelation

Other Abbreviations

AC .... Augsburg Confession

Ap .... Apology of the Augsburg Confession

FC .... Formula of Concord

LC .... Large Catechism

SD .... Solid Declaration of the Formula of Concord

AE .... *Luther's Works*, American Edition

CHAPTER 1

THE GREAT DISCONNECT

Okay. Think fast. What are the first and last books of the Bible? What is the central message of the Bible? How many days did it take for God to create the world? What is the name of the tree that God commanded Adam not to eat from? Where was Adam when his wife ate from the forbidden tree? What happened to Adam and his wife when they ate from the forbidden tree? Where in the Bible is the first promise of a savior? How do Adam, Noah, Abraham, the sacrifice of Isaac, the exodus, the tabernacle, Israel's wandering in the wilderness, Jonah, David, the temple, the Assyrian captivity, and the Babylonian captivity relate to Jesus? Who is Jesus? Why are the cross and empty tomb important? Why did Jesus ascend to heaven? What is so significant about the apostles, Stephen, Philip, Prochorus, Nicanor, Timon, Parmenas, Nicolaus, and Paul? When will Jesus return? What will happen when He does? What will heaven be like? And what does any of this stuff have to do with my daily life?

If you can't answer some, most, or all of these questions, do not feel bad. You are not alone. A recent study conducted by the American Bible Society in conjunction with Barna Group research revealed that while 87 percent of surveyed households own a Bible, and 73 percent professed to be somewhat knowledgeable about the contents of the Bible, only 57 percent knew that Mary Magdalene was the first person to see Jesus after the resurrection. Fifty-six percent knew that Peter was the disciple who denied Jesus. And fewer than 50 percent of surveyed households believed that the Bible is the infallible, inerrant Word of God.[1] Another study revealed that "nearly 26 million Americans reduced or stopped their interaction with Scripture in the past year."[2] What research has discovered, and my own experience as a pastor has revealed, is that Americans, Christians included, are becoming increasingly biblically illiterate. We don't know the basics of the Christian story and how it all connects.

Now, I realize that this statement might sound trivial. I mean, after all, who cares if I know the name of a tree, how many days it took for God to create the world, the first reference to a Savior, or even how Adam, Noah, Abraham, the sacrifice of Isaac, the exodus, the tabernacle, Israel's wandering in the wilderness, Jonah, David, the temple, the Assyrian

---

1 American Bible Society, "State of the Bible 2017," (February 2017): 71–78. https://1s712.americanbible.org/state-of-the-bible/stateofthebible/State_of_the_bible-2017.pdf (accessed July 29, 2022).

2 American Bible Society, "State of the Bible 2022," (January 2022). https://1s712.americanbible.org/state-of-the-bible/stateofthebible/State_of_the_bible-2022.pdf (accessed July 29, 2022).

captivity, and the Babylonian captivity connect to Jesus? As long as I know who Jesus is and what He did for me on the cross and in the empty tomb, isn't that enough? *Isn't that all I need to know to be saved?*

While it is true that all people who confess with their mouth that Jesus is Lord and believe in their heart that God raised Him from the dead will be saved (see Rm 10:9), it is also true that there are great dangers in asking a question like this. The first danger is that the tenor of the question treats the Word of God apathetically. Jesus, however, does not. He eagerly read from the scroll of the prophet Isaiah in the Nazareth synagogue (see Lk 4:17–21). He regularly references the beginning of creation, Adam, Abraham, Moses, David, Israel, and many other Old Testament people and events. He stressed the importance of hearing God's Word when He said, "Whoever is of God hears the words of God" (Jn 8:47). If that were too little, the psalmist proclaims, "Oh how I love Your law! It is my meditation all the day" (Ps 119:97). And Paul commends the entirety of Scripture to Timothy: "All Scripture is breathed out by God and profitable for teaching, for reproof, for correction, and for training in righteousness, that the man of God may be complete, equipped for every good work" (2 Tm 3:16–17).

If that is how our Lord and His patriarchs, prophets, and apostles speak about the Word of God, how can we apathetically say, "Who cares?" We are given to pay close attention to God's Word (see Heb 2:1), lest we drift away from it and find ourselves numbered among the lukewarm Christians God threatened to spit out of His mouth (see Rv 3:16). As Christians, we, like those who have gone before us, should receive God's Word eagerly and examine the Scriptures daily (see Ac 17:11).

The second danger with the question is the words "need to know." Not only does the question approach the faith minimalistically, as if to say, "I have learned all that I need to, so I am good," but it also reduces the faith to mere knowledge and intellect. When that happens, the faith becomes an act of memorizing information, acquiring knowledge, learning facts, and knowing doctrinal content. Sadly, a good number of churches' current modules of Christian formation tend to reinforce this view of the Christian faith.

That is not surprising since, over the past four hundred years, the Church's catechesis, or process of Christian formation, has undergone substantial changes as an effect of the Enlightenment. The Enlightenment's emphasis on reason shifted the focus of the Christian faith away from "the revelation of God's wisdom in the words of Holy Scriptures" and toward "the rationalistic abilities of man."[3] Moreover, the rationalists of the Enlightenment went so far as to alter the classical Evangelical school curriculum, which had traditionally emphasized the authority of the written Word, so that the students would then be more open to new rationalistic teachings and resistant to classical Lutheran orthodoxy.[4] Inevitably, the process and terminology of Christian formation changed from "talking and teaching" to "lectures and instruction." "Formation" gave way to "education." "Home Altars" gave way to "Sunday School," "Confirmation Classes," and "Adult Instruction Classes." "Narrative" gave way to "facts." "Faith" gave way to "knowledge and intellectual assent." The crowning complexity of God's creation, a fearfully and wonderfully made person (Ps 139:14), is treated as a brain on a stick. And a minimalistic attitude toward Christianity comes to say that "when I have learned everything I need to know, then I can be done with Church. Like school, I can graduate, move on, and never return."

Now, please don't misunderstand me. Memorization, knowledge, facts, and doctrinal content are vital to Christian formation and the faith. But when the faith is reduced to mere knowledge, then the unified, overarching story of the biblical narrative from Genesis to Revelation, in which the knowledge, facts, and doctrine of the faith are given, is chopped into disconnected, independent, seemingly unrelated, and trivial pieces. And when you cannot see and know how the story connects, God's story becomes anthropocentric. This means that the faith begins to revolve around you.

The "I" in the question "Isn't that all I need to know to be saved?" is the last and greatest danger. "Why?" you might wonder. I suppose I could simply say that it's idolatry and move on. But I don't think that a two-word answer particularly helps you see the intricacies of that danger on a practical, everyday level. So allow me to illustrate by taking a beloved Scripture passage, sometimes called "the Gospel in a Nutshell," and changing the

---

3   Thomas Korcok, *Lutheran Education: From Wittenberg to the Future* (St. Louis: Concordia Publishing House, 2011), 94.
4   Korcok, *Lutheran Education*, 94.

words so that it becomes all about me: For God so loved me, that He gave His only Son, that if I believe in Him, I will not perish, but I will have eternal life. Compare that to the actual verse: "For God so loved the world, that He gave His only Son, that whoever believes in Him should not perish but have eternal life" (Jn 3:16).

Do you see the difference? Putting myself in the center strips every other person and event from God's story of salvation in Jesus Christ. It disconnects me from God's creation, His people, and His redemptive work for both throughout history, Genesis through Revelation. It makes it seem like the only thing that truly matters to God is me. It discards and disregards my neighbor, even though God has commanded me to "love your neighbor as yourself" (Mk 12:31). It essentially says that everything God has done, is doing, and will do is always only for me. God is here to love, help, bless, care for, protect, and give me whatever I need and want, when I want it and when I need it. In short, the faith becomes a private matter between God and me. And when the faith is privatized, then Christ's Church is no longer seen as a body or community of believers comprised of people of various ages, experiences, ethnicities, languages, and historical eras who weekly gather around Jesus in Word and Sacrament and then daily live their lives in Him. Church is transformed into a place where I go to meet my consumeristic needs or receive some sort of social benefit.

Hence there are many Christians in America who view going to church like they view grocery shopping. They have a list, sometimes an exceptionally long one, of all the things that they need. The list is usually generated from individual relationships, personal interests, hobbies, and goals. So if I am single, I try to find a church that has a large population of single people or a singles group so that I might have companionship or even find my lifelong companion, meaning my spouse. If I have children, I try to find a church that has an abundance of children and offers a top-notch Sunday School, Vacation Bible School, confirmation program, youth group, and young adult group so that they have a good foundation with good Christian friends and lots of fun. If I like mission work, I find a church that is active in local, national, and international mission work. If I have a question, I find a church that can give me the right answer. If I like basketball, softball, quilting, cooking, or hanging out with my fellow men or women; if I want financial stability or need help working on a personal issue, I need a church with those programs. If I want to feel closer to God, I need to find the church with the right style of worship, music, and lively educational opportunities that suit me. The possibilities of the list are seemingly endless, but you get the picture. The church must have what I am looking for. It must meet my needs. If not, I will simply go to the next place until I find one that does.

At the same time, there are many Christians in America who view church like they view attending a family reunion. They attend because they want to connect to their past, catch up with family, or become more well-known, accepted, and loved. So if I want to connect to my past, I attend a particular church because my parents and/or grandparents attended or founded the church. Or I go to Sunday School because my parents sent me, as their parents sent them. If I want to catch up with the latest gossip, I attend because I like and want to talk to a lot of the people, my friends go there, or this is the community church. If I want to become more well-known, accepted, and loved, I attend or simply claim membership in a particular church because this community is a Christian community, and I want to be accepted as part of the community, so I need to belong to a church in it. Or I want to be married and/or buried on the church's property. Again, the possibilities are seemingly endless, and you get the picture. I attend or simply belong to a specific church so that I can honor my familial ties, enjoy social interactions, or become well-known, accepted, and loved in order to receive a specific social benefit.

And while both of these trends can be observed in any context of American Christianity, it has been my experience that cities with urban and suburban settings trend more toward consumeristic Christianity, while small towns and rural settings trend toward social Christianity. Perhaps that is because in a big city's larger urban and suburban environment, you can't know everyone, so you simply get accustomed to walking by and ignoring countless people since you do not know them and perhaps will never meet them again. Whereas in a small town or rural environment, you are expected to know everyone, wave at everyone as you walk or drive by, stop and have a conversation as you shop in the local stores, and gather in the local churches to enjoy social interactions and community events.

Regardless, both are anthropocentric views of the Church that have, at their core, a privatized understanding of the faith. Both inevitably sever me from the true Church, the body of Christ throughout the ages, in which Jesus, the Head (see Col 1:18), promises to be present to forgive sins, strengthen faith, and give eternal life (see Mt 18:20). And through which He daily abides for the life and sake of His creation, the world (see Php 2:13). To be cut off and disconnected from Christ and His Church is ultimately to wither, to die, and to be thrown into the fire and burned (see Jn 15:6).

Suddenly, what once sounded trivial, sounds trivial no longer. It is a matter of life and death. We must once again see that the faith is not something we simply learn, regurgitate, graduate, and move on from. It is not something I fit into my personal story or life for one hour per week on a Sunday morning or whenever I seem to need it. Nor is the faith a private matter between God and me.

We must discover anew that the faith, including the Church, does not revolve around us. It revolves around and is all about Jesus, the Promised Child, who has come to crush the head of the serpent and restore the presence of God to His fallen creation. It is not mere information, knowledge, facts, and doctrinal content to be learned but a life lived in Christ and situated in the context of the unified biblical narrative of divine presence. More profoundly and eloquently stated, the life of a Christian, indeed your life, is firmly rooted and intricately woven into the unified biblical narrative of God's presence in the person and work of Jesus Christ, into whom you were incorporated by Baptism, with whom you abide each week in the Divine Service, and under whom you and all believers will live at the resurrection.

What does this mean? That's a great Lutheran question, and I'm glad I asked it. In order to answer this question, we must first piece together the disconnected, independent, and seemingly unrelated and trivial pieces of Bible stories so that we can see the unified, overarching story of the biblical narrative from Genesis to Revelation.

CHAPTER 2

PIECING IT TOGETHER: FROM EDEN TO EGYPT

Whether you are a lifelong Christian, new to the faith, or somewhere in between, reading the Bible can be challenging. That is not too surprising since the Bible is a compilation of sixty-six books, with over thirty authors who employ different writing styles and literary genres, all the while discussing numerous places and countless names. Our comprehension of it is also impaired by how we typically encounter the biblical narrative. Most people do not sit down and read the Bible from cover to cover. Rather, we pick it up, read a chapter or two, and put it down. We go to church and hear three different readings. We go to Bible study and look at a few verses, a chapter, or perhaps a specific topic. We go to Sunday School and hear a story. Consequently, the biblical narrative tends to become disconnected, and the stories seen as unrelated and independent. It is as if someone marched into the room, dumped a three-thousand-piece puzzle on the table in front of us, enthusiastically proclaimed, "Look at this breathtakingly beautiful picture!" and then walked out of the room with the box in hand. What lies before us may indeed be a breathtakingly beautiful picture, but do you know what I see? Three thousand disconnected individual pieces, each with its own image.

But the pieces are not independent, nor the images unrelated. Rather, each piece connects in a very specific and deliberate way to form a much larger, intricate, and breathtakingly beautiful picture, or in the case of the Bible, a story. And the only way I get to see the picture in all its intricate beauty is if I connect the pieces. And the way to connect the pieces is to use the unified picture on the box as my guide.

Thankfully, when it comes to the Bible, we as Christians still have the picture on the box. Or better yet, we have the unified, overarching story of the biblical narrative. What is the overarching story? In John 5:39, Jesus tells the Jews, "You search the Scriptures because you think that in them you have eternal life; and it is they that bear witness about Me." After the resurrection, Jesus provides Cleopas and another disciple with a more detailed expression of the overarching story when He says, "'O foolish ones, and slow of heart to believe all that the prophets have spoken! Was it not necessary that the Christ should suffer these things and enter into His glory?' And beginning with Moses and all the Prophets, He interpreted to them in all the Scriptures the things concerning Himself" (Lk 24:25–27). But perhaps the clearest and most concise articulation of it is found in

John 20:31: "These are written so that you may believe that Jesus is the Christ, the Son of God, and that by believing you may have life in His name." Essentially, the Bible is all about divine presence, or eternal life with the eternal Lord. Knowing this, let's take these individual puzzle pieces, or stories, that we know and love and connect them to the larger, intricate, overarching biblical narrative of divine presence so that we may see the breathtakingly beautiful story of God's message of salvation for all people, in Jesus Christ, as recorded in Genesis through Revelation, of which our lives, as we shall later see, are also one piece.

"In the beginning, God created the heavens and the earth" (Gn 1:1), the biblical text begins. Whose beginning? God's beginning? No. Note how the text presupposes the existence of God. To be God means that He has no beginning and no end. God is existence. God is life. So much so that out of nothing, He creates and gives life to the heavens and the earth. And He does it in one of the simplest yet most profound ways: through the Word. God says,

> "Let there be light," and there was light. And God saw that the light was good. And God separated the light from the darkness. God called the light Day, and the darkness He called Night. And there was evening and there was morning, the first day. (Gn 1:3–5)

Notice the deliberate ordering of creation: from speaking to creating to separating and naming. Everything is perfect, rightly ordered, and exactly as God wants it. Everything is *good*.

The same deliberate order and purposeful design can be seen throughout the subsequent days of creation. Like a masterful artist dipping his paint-brush into the vibrant colors of the palette and creating initial random shapes and structures, only to return to those shapes one by one and fill them in with intricate detail in a way that inevitably produces a master-piece, so our God creates. On day one, He creates light. On day four, He returns and fills it in with intricate detail: the sun, moon, and stars. On day two, He creates the sky and water. On day five, He places various birds in the sky and aquatic animals in the water. On day three, He creates land and a variety of vegetation. On day six, He creates animals and man to walk on the land and eat the vegetation. For six days, God creates and gives life to the heavens and the earth by the power of His Word. And having completed everything, knowing that it is finished, He rests on the seventh day.

The focus of this story, however, is not simply creation. Rather, it is the creation of man and woman and their relationship with God. This is evident by the fact that the biblical narrative revisits the work of God on days three and six in Genesis 2. It emphasizes that God intimately and intentionally formed man's body out of the dust of the ground and breathed into his nostrils the breath of life. Man is created, body and soul. The woman is formed from his side. Both are created in the image of God, and each one is given a unique responsibility of caring for God's creation. But what is more, God is present with them in the land that He created. He is in their midst. It is paradise. There is no illness, disease, mourning, crying, pain, or death. There is simply eternal life with the eternal Lord.

But in Genesis 3, there is a big problem. The serpent who had sinned (see 1Jn 3:8; 2Pt 2:4; Mt 25:41) and who hates God's created order speaks to the woman. She listens to the serpent and trusts his word. She eats of the fruit and gives some to her husband, who is standing there with her (see Gn 3:6). He listens to the voice of his wife, who is echoing the voice of the serpent, and eats. And in one act, Adam and his wife sin. They disobey God and eat from the tree of the knowledge of good and evil that they are commanded not to eat from. And the result is not merely that they sinned and that creation is corrupted. No, in fact, it has a much greater and more profound effect, namely that this corruption brings the punishment of death. Not just a physical or temporal death where the heart stops beating and the lungs stop drawing breath, but an eternal death, a separation from the holy and perfect God. The man and the woman lose God's face-to-face, unveiled presence. They are exiled from the land and can no longer walk with, talk with, or see God in the same way.[5] For a sinner cannot stand in the presence of God and live (see Ex 33:20; Ps 5:4; Is 6:5).

However, the hope of eternal life in God's presence is not lost. For God "is not a God of the dead, but of the living" (Mk 12:27). And He does not delight "in the death of the wicked" (Ezk 18:23). So God speaks a word of promise and restoration, the *protoevangelium*. In Genesis 3:15, He says to the serpent, "I will put enmity between you and the woman, and between

---

5 For a detailed account of this, see Gn 3:23–24.

your offspring and her offspring; He shall [crush] your head, and you shall bruise His heel."[6] In other words, I know that Adam and his wife have befriended you, Satan, and made themselves My enemies. But I am going to do something about that. I am going to do what they are incapable of doing. I am going to cause a division and separation to occur between you and the woman. I am going to send a Promised Seed of the woman, a child, who will crush your head and restore to them the promised land, My eternal presence.

Adam's belief and trust in God's promise is evidenced by the naming of his wife. In Genesis 3:20, after hearing God's judgment of death—"For you are dust, and to dust shall you return" (Gn 3:19), Adam responds not by naming his wife "the mother of the dead ones," but rather, he names her Eve, "because she was the mother of all living."

Consequently, though Adam and Eve are banished from God's face-to-face, unveiled presence, the promise of restoration remains. And the rest of the Old Testament can be understood and summarized by this promise of divine presence. That is, we, like Adam and Eve, are left wondering, "Where is this Promised Child who is going to crush the head of the serpent and restore to us the presence of God?"

Given the nature of God's promise, it is not surprising that Genesis 4 begins with the birth of a child, upon whose delivery Eve exclaims, "I have gotten the man of the Lord."[7] But neither Cain nor Abel are the Promised Child since Cain murders his brother and is sentenced to live a nomadic life even further "away from the presence of the LORD" (Gn 4:16). Additionally, the Promised Child cannot come from Cain's family tree since, at the end of chapter 4, we see Cain's great-great-great-grandson, Lamech, pridefully boast about killing someone who injured him.

Genesis 5 begins in a rather strange way. "When God created man, He made him in the likeness of God. Male and female He created them, and He blessed them and named them Man when they were created" (Gn 5:1–2). Wait a minute! What is going on? Is this another creation account? Is God creating another world or the world anew? No. God must appoint

---

6   Brackets indicate the author's translation.

7   Martin Luther, *Luther's Works*, American Edition, vol. 1: *Lectures on Genesis: Chapters 1–5*, ed. J. J. Pelikan, H. C. Oswald, and H. T. Lehmann, (St. Louis: Concordia Publishing House, 1999), 241. For Luther's full discussion of this, read the context of *Luther's Works*, vol. 1, 241–43.

another (see Gn 4:25). Hence the language reflects that of Genesis 1 and 2, but the focus remains on the Promised Child. And while God's people have many "other sons and daughters,"[8] Scripture's focus is on one specific name for each generation. The list in chapter 5 ends with Noah, of whom it is said, "Out of the ground that the LORD has cursed, this one shall bring us relief" (Gn 5:29).

But in Noah's lifetime, the separation of humanity from God reaches a climactic point as divine judgment in the form of a flood rains down upon all of humanity for forty days and forty nights because "the wickedness of man was great . . . every intention of the thoughts of his heart was only evil continually" (Gn 6:5). One by one, all of creation, including man, is swept away by raging waters since the "wages of sin is death" (Rm 6:23). And what became of God's promise? It remained. God instructed believing Noah to build an ark so that by it, He might save not only pairs of every kind of animal but also Noah and his family, "eight persons" (1Pt 3:20) in all. Tragically, though, after emerging from the ark about a year later, receiving God's promise to never again destroy the earth by a flood, and then building an altar and worshiping the Lord, Noah was found to be lying naked and in a drunken stupor. Since Noah turns out not to be the one to bring us relief, there must be another descendant who will crush the head of the serpent and restore the presence of God.

Noah's son Ham[9] is disqualified since he receives a curse for uncovering his father's nakedness (see Gn 9:20–27). Japheth is also disqualified since his blessing from Noah specifically speaks of dwelling "in the tents of Shem" (Gn 9:27). Shem is the one who carries the promise given to Adam after humanity's fall into sin. Therefore, just like in Genesis 5, Scripture's focus, as it recounts Shem's genealogy, is on one specific name for each generation. Yet in the middle of this recounting of Shem's family tree, there is a break that occurs. During the time of Peleg, "the earth was divided" (Gn 10:25). Once again, sinful man refuses to listen to the word

---

8   This phrase runs like a refrain through Genesis. Since none are mentioned by name, this phrase appears to be used to further emphasize the importance of the specific male child who is given the promise of divine presence spoken to Adam in Gn 3:15. In the same way, the repetition of "and he died" demonstrates both a continuation of God's promise from one generation to the next and a fulfillment of God's judgment of death upon human sin.

9   Some of Ham's descendants would later become known as the Canaanites, whom Noah had already pronounced a curse upon in Gn 9:25.

of the Lord: "Be fruitful and multiply, increase greatly on the earth and multiply in it" (Gn 9:7). They did not want to be dispersed "over the face of all the earth" (Gn 11:8). They wanted to make a name for themselves. So they disobediently built a city and a tower. It was named Babel because the Lord came down and, as a punishment, confused their language to the degree that they could not understand one another and then dispersed the people. What is absolutely crucial about the break in Shem's family tree is that it indicates that Peleg is the descendant of Shem, who will carry the promise given to Adam.

Only five generations after this, God appears and speaks to Peleg's insignificant[10] pagan[11] of a great-great-great-grandson, Abram. God tells Abram, "Go from your country and your kindred and your father's house to the land that I will show you. And I will make of you a great nation, and I will bless you and make your name great, so that you will be a blessing. I will bless those who bless you, and him who dishonors you I will curse, and in you all the families of the earth shall be blessed" (Gn 12:1–3). What is absolutely remarkable is not simply that God appears and tells a nobody that He will make his name great, but rather, in appearing and speaking to a nobody, God speaks a promise that concerns more than just Abram and his family, who would later become the nation of Israel. God speaks a promise that encompasses "all families of the earth" or all the people. But how exactly will all people be blessed through Abram? Over the next three chapters, God reveals that it will be through Abram's descendants (see 12:7; 13:14–17), more specifically an offspring or son.[12] So while there are a few specific nuances of Abram's promise that are only applicable to him, the promise itself is nothing new. It is a continuation of God's promise to Adam to send a Promised Child who is going to crush the head of the serpent and restore to us the presence of God.

Nearly ten years later however, at the start of chapter 16, Abram's wife Sarai despairs that the promise of God is yet to be fulfilled. She is still

---

10 Abram would have had very little status in the ancient world since, as Gn 11:27–23 states, he is nomadic after his brother Haran died, his wife is barren, and his father, Terah, dies not long after leaving Ur for Haran.

11 Jsh 24:2 specifically notes that Terah, and thus his household, who were living "beyond the Euphrates" in Ur, "served other gods."

12 See Gn 15:3–4, 13–14. Additionally, Gal 3:16 specifically names Christ as the fulfillment of God's promise to Abram of an offspring.

barren! Consequently, Sarai encourages Abram to take matters into his own hands and procreate with her servant Hagar, who later gives birth to Ishmael. Ishmael, however, is not the Promised Child, as his blessing (see Gn 16:11–12) is antithetical to Adam's promise. God even refuses to give the promise to Ishmael and insists that Abram's wife, Sarai, will bear a son, Isaac, through whom He will establish His everlasting covenant (see Gn 17:18–19). To confirm this and give them certainty of the promise in the midst of both natural and postmenopausal barrenness,[13] God even goes so far as renaming Abram to Abraham and Sarai to Sarah. And it is a good thing He confirms His promise because Abraham and Sarah have waited twenty-five years before Isaac is born.[14]

Perhaps even more shocking, only twenty-seven verses later, in what seems to be a very gut-wrenching turn of events, God tells Abraham, "Take your son, your only son Isaac, whom you love, and go to the land of Moriah, and offer him there as a burnt offering on one of the mountains of which I shall tell you" (Gn 22:2). Yet more ghastly, Abraham saddles his donkey. He lays the wood for the sacrifice on Isaac's back. Isaac carries the wood on which he will die up the mountain. Abraham takes the wood that Isaac was carrying, lays it on the altar he built, binds his beloved and only son to it, and sets out to kill him. What? Kill the beloved and only son? What about God's promise of divine presence?

Well, the good news is Isaac does not die. God prevents Abraham from sacrificing his only beloved son. Instead, God provides a ram for sacrifice in his place (see Gn 22:13). And if that gift and blessing were too little, in chapter 24, God even provides a wife for Isaac. Isaac and Rebekah are truly a match made in heaven. Though Isaac has never met her, Abraham's servant, who is sent to find a wife for Isaac, prays a very specific prayer that is answered by God verbatim. And Rebekah receives a blessing from her family, which parallels the promise of divine presence given to Isaac by the Lord (see Gn 24:60; 22:18).

In chapter 25, Rebekah gives birth to two sons, Esau and Jacob. Esau should be the one who will carry the promise since he is the firstborn. However, God tells Rebekah that this will not happen, as "the older shall

---

13 According to Gn 17:17, Sarah is ninety years old when she becomes pregnant.
14 According to Gn 12:4, Abram was seventy-five years old when God made the promise to Abram. And in Gn 21:5, he is one hundred years old when Isaac is born.

serve the younger" (Gn 25:23). Not surprising then, Esau dramatically sells his birthright to Jacob for lentil stew and bread. But before any promise is passed to Jacob, a famine arises that forces Isaac and his family to leave the land and travel to Gerar. And because God knows sinful humanity and our weakness of unbelief, He beautifully reiterates the promise so that Isaac can cling to the word of God during his sojourning. God declares to Isaac that his offspring will inherit the land, God will dwell with them, and they shall be numerous (see Gn 26:2–5). Having successfully survived the famine and settled in the land of Shibah, Isaac passes the promise to Jacob, who slyly claims it.[15]

But actions have consequences. As a result of Jacob's deception, he is forced to leave the land of Canaan, which God swore Jacob would inherit and where He would be with him. Jacob flees Beersheba to live with his uncle Laban in Haran. Along the way, however, Jacob has a rather peculiar dream. Since the sun has set, Jacob decides to spend the night in what he later calls Bethel, meaning the "house of God" (Gn 28:17). And he calls it that because as he is sleeping, he sees "a ladder set up on the earth, and the top of it reached to heaven. And behold, the angels of God were ascending and descending on it!" (Gn 28:12). Directly above the ladder stands the Lord, who proclaims, "I am the LORD, the God of Abraham your father and the God of Isaac. The land on which you lie I will give to you and to your offspring. Your offspring shall be like the dust of the earth, and you shall spread abroad to the west and to the east and to the north and to the south, and in you and your offspring shall all the families of the earth be blessed" (Gn 28:13–14).

After hearing how, yet again, God is going to send the Promised Child who is going to crush the head of the serpent and restore to us the presence of God, Jacob departs to Haran. During his time there, he marries two sisters, Leah and Rachel, and has twelve sons: Reuben, Simeon, Levi, Judah, Dan, Naphtali, Gad, Asher, Issachar, Zebulun, Joseph, and Benjamin (see Gn 35:23–26). And in chapter 35, as he returns to Canaan with them, Jacob gets into a little tussle. He wrestles until dawn with God, who dislocates hip. Jacob, however, continues to struggle against God, insisting that, "I will not let You go unless You bless me" (Gn 32:26). God acquiesces to his request and renames him Israel in confirmation of the promise of

---

15 See Gn 27.

divine presence.

Subsequently, chapter 37 focuses on Joseph and his dreams. And in truth, of all of Israel's twelve sons, it looks like Joseph will be the one who will receive the promise. After all, the remaining chapters up through Genesis 48 deal primarily with Joseph, who is sold into slavery, rescued from prison, and appointed as Pharaoh's right hand to save Egypt from the coming famine. "All," that is, except one.

In chapter 38, only one chapter into this story, we get the narrative of Judah and Tamar. Now it would be tempting to see this story as a seemingly disconnected, independent, haphazard piece of the puzzle that only draws our attention away from the Joseph narrative. And it would be easy to ask why this story is even included. But again, the Bible is not a bunch of disconnected and independent stories. So the question to ask is, "How does this all connect to the promise of divine presence?"

Genesis 44 answers that question for us. In a surprising turn of events, Joseph's brothers (who had thrown him into a pit, sold him into slavery, and then dipped his robe in blood to convince their father he was dead) are now unknowingly bowing before him and asking him, a supposed stranger, to provide food for them so that they can survive the famine. Joseph does provide them with food, but not before devising a plan to test them and see if they turned from their wickedness. He places his silver cup in the food sack of his brother Benjamin. After sending his brothers on their way home with the food, Joseph orders his guards to chase and seize his brothers, accusing them of stealing his silver cup. Dumbfounded by Joseph's accusation, the brothers protest, "How then could we steal silver or gold from your lord's house? Whichever of your servants is found with it shall die, and we also will be my lord's servants" (Gn 44:8–9). After readily lowering their food sacks for Joseph to search, it is revealed that Benjamin has the cup. And rather than putting them all into servitude, Joseph divulges, "Only the man in whose hand the cup was found shall be my servant" (Gn 44:17). Judah, out of love for his father and brother, offers to give up his freedom and life for Benjamin. He will stay and suffer for sins he did not commit so that Benjamin may go free.

In this one great sacrificial act of love, we see a foreshadowing of Gn 49:8–10, where Jacob passes the promise to Judah, saying:

> **Judah, your brothers shall praise you;**
> > **your hand shall be on the neck of your enemies;**
> > **your father's sons shall bow down before you.**
>
> **Judah is a lion's cub;**
> > **from the prey, my son, you have gone up.**
>
> **He stooped down; he crouched as a lion**
> > **and as a lioness; who dares rouse him?**
>
> **The scepter shall not depart from Judah,**
> > **nor the ruler's staff from between his feet,**
> > **until tribute comes to him;**
> > **and to him shall be the obedience of the peoples.**

That answer might sound very strange. In fact, you may even be wondering, Why did we just spend ten chapters on Joseph if Judah receives the promise of divine presence? Well, without Joseph, the promise of a child who will crush the head of the serpent and restore the presence of God would have ended since Judah would have died of starvation. Hence, after the death of his father, Jacob, Joseph says to his brothers, "As for you, you meant evil against me, but God meant it for good, to bring it about that many people should be kept alive, as they are today. So do not fear; I will provide for you and your little ones" (Gn 50:20–21).

As joyous as that sounds and as much as I would love to tell you that is the conclusion and the happy ending to God's story, I can't. The end of Genesis presents a rather big problem. The Israelites are no longer in the Promised Land. They are in Egypt, where Joseph brought them all. Additionally, Judah was only given the promise of a child. He is not the Promised Child. So, by the end of Genesis, the promise, spoken to Adam so long ago in the Garden of Eden, remains unfulfilled. And the Israelites are left waiting and wondering, "Where is this Promised Child who is going to crush the head of the serpent and restore to us the presence of God?"

And so, the biblical narrative continues into the Book of Exodus. However, at the start of the book, we learn that a significant complication to the fulfillment of God's promise has occurred. After the death of Joseph, a new pharaoh has risen to power who "did not know Joseph" (Ex 1:8).

What he did know, however, was that Israel and his twelve sons had been fruitful and multiplied. What started as a large family quickly grew into a nation. Pharaoh was so terrified of losing power and being dethroned that he decided to enslave the Israelites before they could think of joining an invading enemy army in battle and overthrowing him. With the nation of Israel now enslaved, they were unable to travel to the land God had promised to give them and dwell with them (see Gn 26:3).

For over four hundred years, Israel bitterly labored under the oppressive hand of Pharaoh, either tending to the fields or constructing the Egyptians' buildings. Pharaoh even sought to reduce their population by ordering Israelite midwives to kill all male Israelite infants upon birth. However, God protected them through the hands of the midwives as they secretly refused to carry out Pharaoh's orders. More than that, God remembered His people, the Israelites, who were groaning and crying out for help, by sending them a deliverer to free them from Egyptian slavery.

Specifically, God appeared to Moses, an Israelite, from the tribe of Levi, who himself had barely escaped death twice. First, when his mother subverted Pharaoh's edict, placing the three-month-old in an ark[16] in the reeds of the Nile. There, Pharaoh's daughter found poor, helpless baby Moses as she bathed, took him into her house, and raised him as her own. And second, when Moses fled Egypt to Midian in fear of death, having killed an Egyptian taskmaster for beating a fellow Israelite. Upon appearing to Moses in a burning bush and declaring, "I am the God of your father, the God of Abraham, the God of Isaac, and the God of Jacob" (Ex 3:6), God demands that Moses appear before Pharaoh so that the Israelites, God's "firstborn son," might be freed from Egyptian slavery and finally inherit the land that He promised them and in which He will dwell (Ex 4:22).

But a stubborn and hard-hearted Pharaoh refuses to listen to the word of the Lord as proclaimed by Moses. And as we have seen before, "the wages of sin is death" (Rm 6:23). So God enacts a series of divine judgments upon Pharaoh and Egypt in the form of ten plagues, as shown in Figure 1.

The tenth and final plague is the last straw. For in the tenth plague, the Lord "will go out in the midst of Egypt, and every firstborn in the land

---

16 The Hebrew word הַבַּת, which appears in Ex 2:3, is the same word that appears and is used in Gn 6:14–9:18 to describe the ark Noah was to build and live in during the time of the flood.

Plagues as Judgment on the False Gods of Egypt

PLAGUE	EGYPTIAN GOD TARGETED
1. Nile is turned to blood	**Khnum:** creator of water and life **Hapi:** Nile god **Osiris:** the Nile was his bloodstream
2. Frogs	**Heket:** goddess of childbirth whose symbol was the frog
3. Gnats	**Amon-Ra:** the creator and king of the gods; had the head of a beetle
4. Flies	**Amon-Ra:** the creator and king of the gods, had the head of a beetle
5. Livestock	**Hathor:** mother and sky goddess whose symbol was the cow **Apis:** bull god
6. Boils	**Imhotep:** god of medicine
7. Hail	**Seth:** god of wind and storm
8. Locusts	**Isis:** goddess of life **Min:** goddess of fertility and vegetation; protector of crops
9. Darkness	**Amon, Re, Atum, Horus:** sun gods
10. Death of the firstborn	**Osiris:** judges of the dead and patron deity of the pharaoh

Figure 1a: Plagues of Egypt

of Egypt shall die, from the firstborn of Pharaoh who sits on his throne, even to the firstborn of the slave girl who is behind the handmill, and all the firstborn of the cattle" (Ex 11:4–5). Wait. Every firstborn in the land of Egypt? What about Israel? What about the promise of divine presence?

Well, God saves Israel in a way that is somewhat reminiscent of how He spared Isaac from Abraham. God tells Moses and the Israelites to

The Five Purposes of the Plagues:

1. To free Israel from slavery.

2. To punish Egypt for the oppression of Israel and give an opportunity for repentance and faith (see Is 19).

3. To demonstrate the foolishness of idolatry.

4. To reveal the nature of the divine name and who He is (see Ex 6:3).

5. To demonstrate that God is the Creator. Only the Creator can exercise such power over his creation (water, frogs, livestock, Egyptians, and so on).

Figure 1b: Plagues of Egypt

take a male lamb, without blemish or defect, slaughter it at twilight, and smear its blood on the doorframes of their houses. Then, when the Lord passes through the land and executes His judgment of death upon the Egyptians, He will see the blood of the lamb and pass over their houses (see Ex 12:23). No plague shall befall them. By the blood of a lamb, Israel will pass over from death to life! To commemorate this momentous salvific event, God institutes a memorial meal, the Passover, by which they may annually remember how the Lord freed them from Egyptian slavery so that He might fulfill His promise spoken to Adam in the garden long ago. The meal itself consists of bitter herbs, unleavened bread, and lamb, which is to be roasted without breaking any of its bones (see Ex 12:3–11). And each specific food is to be used by the father of the household to tell the story of God's salvation for them. By the end of the meal, generation after generation will know and celebrate that God quickly (unleavened bread) and mightily freed them from bitter slavery in Egypt (bitter herbs) by executing a plague of death on all the firstborn in the land of Egypt. But they were saved from divine judgment of death, passing over from death to life by the blood of a lamb (roasted lamb) (see Ex 11:1; 12:11–13, 26–27; 13:8–15).

So God enacted the final plague of divine judgment upon Egypt and their gods. At midnight, the Lord passed through the land and struck down every firstborn animal and man, including Pharaoh's own son. Israel, however, was saved by the blood of the lamb. And because of God's mighty hand, that very hour Pharaoh sent Israel out of Egypt with flocks, herds, and plundered Egyptian silver, gold, and clothing. And that night, something changed concerning God's promise of divine presence.

CHAPTER 3

PIECING IT TOGETHER: THE RED SEA TO THE PROMISED LAND

What changed that great and glorious Passover evening was of inestimable and unfathomable importance for the people of God. After 430 years (see Ex 12:40–41) of being stuck in Egypt, with no hope of God's promise being fulfilled, the people of God finally set out from Egypt. However, this time they set out not because God had merely appeared to them and told them to go as He did to Abraham at Haran or Moses at Sinai in the burning bush. No! For the first time since Adam and Eve's banishment in the Garden of Eden, God came to dwell with His people physically. He came veiled, in a pillar of cloud by day and a pillar of fire by night, to lead His people to the land that He swore—to Abraham, Isaac, and Jacob—to give them. That night, God and His people departed from Egypt to journey to the place where they were to live together in peace and security permanently.

Their journey to the Promised Land, however, was anything but peaceful and secure. In a fit of panic and fear, Pharaoh changed his mind and chased after Israel with his army, including six hundred of Egypt's elite war chariots and horses. With the prospect of either drowning in the Red Sea or being slaughtered and enslaved by Pharaoh and his army, Israel sarcastically cried, "Is it because there are not graves in Egypt that you have taken us away to die in the wilderness?" (Ex 14:11). But what Israel failed to believe—and hard-hearted Pharaoh underestimated—is that when God makes a promise, He keeps it. His Word is trustworthy and true. So much so that as Pharaoh attacked, Israel needed only to be silent. While Moses stretched out his hands, God divided the waters of the Red Sea by a mighty east wind. And the Lord led Israel—in a pillar of cloud by day and a pillar of fire by night—through the sea on dry ground, causing Pharaoh and his army to pursue. Yet much to their surprise, panic, and horror, as their chariot wheels began to clog and drive heavily in the mud, they cried, "Let us flee from before Israel, for the LORD fights for them against the Egyptians" (Ex 14:25). But it was too late. With Israel safe on the shore, Moses stretched out his hands once again, and God caused the sea to swallow the Egyptian army whole as the waters returned to normal. Thus, God drowned the army of hard-hearted Pharaoh. Yet He led Israel through the waters of the Red Sea on dry ground.

After witnessing this, you would think that Israel would rejoice in peace and security, gladly fearing, loving, and trusting in God,[17] who was with them. And for a brief time, they did. They sang and danced as they stood on the banks of the Red Sea: "I will sing to the LORD, for He has triumphed gloriously; the horse and his rider He has thrown into the sea" (Ex 15:1). But they, like their forefather Adam after the fall into sin, are now slaves to sin. They are "by nature sinful and unclean."[18] So their singing gave way to mourning, and their security gave way to doubt and unbelief. Because while they had the gold and silver they plundered from the Egyptians, they did not have, nor could they find, food or drinkable water. Hence, once again, faithless Israel sarcastically grumbled and cried out against God and Moses, not once, not twice, but three times in a little over a month as they journeyed through the wilderness of Shur, Marah, Elim, and the wilderness of Sin. Their grumbling was so poignant that a place near Rephidim, Massah and Meribah, is named after it.[19] It is there that the people of Israel contentiously cried, "Is the LORD among us or not?" (Ex 17:7).

But God is among His people, albeit veiled, and He will not renege His promise of divine presence. Though they do not deserve it, God remains faithful to His word of promise and provides manna or bread, and He provides water, first through a log thrown into the bitter waters of Marah, and then out of a rock at Horeb (see Ex 15:22–17:7).

As the Lord promised, Israel's first major stop on their journey to the Promised Land was the base of Mount Sinai (see Ex 3:12). In Exodus 19, we see God's fervent desire to speak to and dwell with His people intensify, as the Lord comes down to meet with them (see Ex 19:17). But there are limits and rules for their meeting: not going up the mountain, not touching it, consecrating themselves, and washing their garments, and so on. Why? Because sinners cannot stand in the presence of a holy God and live. So, on the third day, when the people draw near to God, they begin to tremble in fear as they saw the lightning, smoke, and fire from the thick cloud and hear God's voice thunder and the trumpet blast. "You speak to us, and we will listen; but do not let God speak to us, lest we die" (Ex 20:19), they cry out to Moses. And only a small group of Israel's leaders—Moses, Aaron,

---

17 *Concordia: The Lutheran Confessions,* second edition. (St. Louis: Concordia Publishing House, 2006), 317.

18 *LSB,* p. 151.

19 הַסָּם (Massah) is a Hebrew word that means "test." הַמְּרִיבָה (Meribah) is a Hebrew word that means "quarrel."

Nadab, Abihu, and seventy elders—are invited to a brief meeting with God. There, they eat and drink in the presence of God. But only because God mercifully does not "lay His hand" of judgment on these sinners (Ex 24:11). Soon after the meal, everyone must depart from God's presence. No one could remain, except Moses. Only he is invited to come up the mountain and enter the cloud of God's presence.

Taking his assistant Joshua with him, Moses ascends the mountain to receive the Ten Commandments written by God on two "tablets of stone" (Ex 31:18). But Moses does not simply receive the Ten Commandments. Over the course of forty days and forty nights, God does not just hand Moses two tablets of stone that articulate how He designed this world to function back when He created it and how He continues to desire His people to live according to His design. No. This story, God's story, indeed Christianity itself, cannot be reduced to mere morality, to rules and regulations for living. It is all about God dwelling with His people. "So, what else does Moses receive?" you might be wondering. He receives the verbal command and blueprints to make a *tabernacle*, or tent.

I know, a tent doesn't sound all that great or glorious. But this tent was to be constructed using the most elaborate and luxurious materials: gold, silver, bronze, blue yarn, purple yarn, scarlet yarn, fine linens, goats' hair, rams' skins, acacia wood, olive oil, incense, onyx stones, and precious gems. And what if I told you that it contained the most elegant, intricate, and beautiful furnishings: an ark, a table, and an altar of incense all made from the deep and rich brown, fine-grained, distinctively ring-patterned hardwood of an acacia tree and then overlaid with pure gold? Also, it contained a golden seven-branched lampstand that resembled a sweet intoxicatingly fragrant almond tree with all its cups, flowers, and buds (see Ex 25:31–36) and fine twined white linen walls embroidered with images of cherubim woven from the blue, purple, and scarlet yarns. And a special curtain or veil, which mimicked the wall pattern but stretched the full width of the tabernacle, divided it into two separate rooms: the Holy Place and the Most Holy Place.

However, what made the tabernacle elaborate and luxurious was not the materials from which it was constructed or the furnishings which it housed but its use and purpose. This roughly forty-five-foot long, fifteen-foot wide and high, two-roomed tent was to be a "sanctuary" for God that

He might dwell in the midst of His people (see Ex 25:8). Thus, all the elaborate materials, exquisite furnishings, and beautiful tapestry worked to proclaim this one important reality. God now dwells with His people! Hence, the ark of the covenant, the only furnishing located behind the veil in the Most Holy Place, was the place where God sat on His mercy seat enthroned between the cherubim. The table was the place of the bread of the Presence, twelve loaves of fresh baked bread which recounted how God continually provided life-sustaining food for all twelve tribes of Israel on their journey to Sinai and how they now had close-table fellowship with God, just as Moses and the elders had eaten a meal in the presence of God. The altar of incense that filled the Holy Place with smoke reminded them that they were entering into God's presence, like they had witnessed the first time at the base of Mount Sinai. The tree-like lampstand, which had a shape reminiscent of the tree of life in the Garden of Eden and fire reminiscent of the burning bush, filled the Holy Place with resplendent light. The finely woven angelic tapestries located on the earthly walls and the veil of the tabernacle poignantly proclaimed that heaven and earth are full of God's glory.

This is what God was busy revealing to Moses and commanding him to build during those forty days and forty nights on Mount Sinai. Moses was to build a sort of heaven on earth, a place where God "will dwell among the people of Israel and will be their God" (Ex 29:45).

But while God was speaking to Moses about fulfilling His promise of divine presence, faithless Israel was busy speaking to Aaron about making idols. "Up," they cried, "make us gods who shall go before us. As for this Moses, the man who brought us up out of the land of Egypt, we do not know what has become of him" (Ex 32:1). Even though Israel had been freed from Egyptian slavery, led through the Red Sea and the wilderness, and had drawn near to God at the base of Mount Sinai in fewer than forty days, Israel's doubt and unbelief were manifested once again. Like a dog returning to its own vomit or a pig wallowing in its own muddy filth, so Israel returned to the sin of their fathers, to the sin of Adam. They commit idolatry. They break the First Commandment. They want another god. And perhaps more tragically, Aaron, who had previously eaten and drunk with God, obeyed not God's will but man's. He took some of the gold that the Israelites had plundered from the Egyptians and fashioned a golden calf out of it. And when the people saw it, they exclaimed, "These are your gods, O Israel, who brought you up out of the land of Egypt!" (Ex 32:4).

Just as sin separated God from His people in the garden, so it continues to separate them from Him at Sinai. "Go down," the Lord said to Moses, "for your people, whom you brought up out of the land of Egypt, have corrupted themselves. . . . Now therefore let Me alone, that My wrath may burn hot against them, and I may consume them, in order that I may make a great nation out of you" (Ex 32:7,10). Sin has its consequences. The wages of sin is death. So that day, Moses descended the mountain, broke the tablets of stone into pieces, burned the calf that they had made, ground it up into powder, scattered the powder in water, made the people drink it, and then put three thousand idolatrous Israelites to death by the sword of the Levites. And God sent a plague upon Israel, which had sinned against Him.

Yet despite the bleak picture of God's judgment upon Israel's sin, the prevailing word for the people at the base of Mount Sinai was not one of justice and wrath but of mercy. Before Moses descends the mountain, he pleads with God to remember the promise He spoke to Abraham, Isaac, and Jacob (Israel). And when Moses ascends the mountain again, he intercedes and advocates for the people. He asks the Lord to forgive Israel's sin and to allow him to see the glory of God's presence. God is gracious and allows Moses to see His glory, albeit not fully. Moses only sees His back. For sinners cannot stand in the Lord's presence and live (see Ex 33:20). But God is merciful, long-suffering, abounding in steadfast love and faithfulness (see Ex 34:6–7). He forgives Israel, allows Moses to chisel out two new tablets of stone, and then reiterates His promise to drive out the current inhabitants of the Promised Land and dwell with His people in the land He swore He would give to Abraham's offspring.

This time, when Moses descends the mountain, his face shines with the glory of God's presence. He tells the people everything that the Lord had spoken to him, including what was written on the two tablets of stone, the observance of the Sabbath Day, and the building of the tabernacle. And after the tabernacle has been built, inspected, blessed, and anointed with oil, God come down, and His presence fills the mercy seat in the tabernacle, just as He had promised. However, one big problem remains. God is holy, and they are sinners. Therefore, as long as the Lord's presence fills the tabernacle, neither Moses nor the people are allowed to enter the tabernacle and come near to God. So while a profound change had occurred with respect to God's promise of divine presence since God dwells in their midst, there still exists a definitive separation between God and His people. God remains inaccessible to them. He remains veiled, behind a curtain, in the Most Holy Place of the tabernacle. No Israelites allowed.

How is Israel going to talk with God if Moses has no access to Him? How are they going to travel to the Promised Land if they cannot come near the tent even to disassemble it? What about the promise of Genesis 3:15? Will God remain faithful to His Word or not? The questions abound. But God does not leave His people in uncertainty when it comes to His promises, nor is He unfaithful to His Word. This is precisely why, when speaking about the construction of the tabernacle on Mount Sinai, God tells Moses that he will need to consecrate and ordain Aaron and his sons from the Levitical tribe to serve as priests in the tabernacle. Through these priests, God would remove sin from His people. He would sanctify them, or make them holy, so that they could live in His holy presence and have access to Him. And that meant sacrifice.

Daily and on specific occasions, the priests offered five distinct and vital sacrifices as God commanded: a burnt offering, a grain offering, a peace offering, a sin offering, and a guilt offering. Except for the grain offering and peace offerings, which were about thanking God and rejoicing in His good gifts through food and fellowship with Him, sacrifices were mostly about dealing with sin. In fact, twice a day, morning and evening, the priests would offer a burnt offering in which they would slaughter an unblemished animal and then present it to God by sprinkling its blood upon the altar of burnt offering. Then they burned the rest of the animal on this same altar, which was located outside of the tabernacle in the courtyard. Similarly, for the specific sins committed knowingly or unknowingly by individuals and families, the priests would slaughter an unblemished animal and then present it to God by sprinkling its blood upon the altar of burnt offering and pouring the rest of the blood at its base. And for specific sins committed knowingly or unknowingly by the nation of Israel, the priests would slaughter an unblemished animal and then present it to God by entering into the tabernacle's Holy Place, sprinkling its blood seven times before the veil, putting some of the blood on the horns of the altar of incense and pouring the rest of it out at the base of the altar of burnt offering (see Lv 4:13–18). All of this was done to make atonement for the entire nation of Israel. In other words, through this substitutionary, sacrificial offering of blood, God gave sinners His acceptance, pardon, cleansing from sin, and access to His presence.

And while a variety of unblemished animals could and were used in the atoning sacrifices (such as a young bull, a cow, a pigeon, or a turtledove), the animal that was predominantly used was a lamb. The use of the lamb was pivotal in Israel's daily atonement and life with God.

In addition to the daily atoning sacrifices, God instituted a yearly Day of Atonement. Once a year, only Aaron, the high priest, and later his successors, was allowed to enter the Most Holy Place without fear of death and make atonement for all of Israel. First, the high priest created a thick cloud of smoke with the altar of incense in the Holy Place. Then he entered behind the veil into the Most Holy Place and brought with him the blood of a bull to atone for his own sin and the blood of a goat to atone for Israel's. He sprinkled the blood of the bull on the front of the east side of the Mercy Seat seven times. And then he sprinkled the blood of the goat on the Mercy Seat and in front of the mercy seat seven times. He would then move to the Holy Place and sprinkle the blood seven times before the veil and put some of the blood on the horns of the altar of incense, just like he did when presenting a sin offering. After this, he would leave the tabernacle and enter the courtyard, where God promised to meet with His people. He would anoint the horns of the altar of burnt offering and sprinkle the blood on the altar seven times. Finally, the high priest would lay his hands on the head of a second goat, confess Israel's sins over it, and send it out into the wilderness, never to return. This occurred annually so that all of Israel's sins were removed from them and the tabernacle was cleansed of the "uncleanness" it had incurred while dwelling in the midst of sinful Israel (see Lv 16:16–19, 30).

However, before Aaron and his sons could do any of this, before they could enter the tabernacle and serve as priests in the presence of a holy God, they first had to be sanctified. And so did their vestments, or clothes, that they were to wear when they were inside the tabernacle.

So Moses assembled the congregation of Israel in the courtyard.

He washed Aaron and the rest of the priests with water and clothed them in their vestments, which consisted of a checkered coat, a sash, a robe, an ephod with a woven band, a breast piece, and a turban. Each of these vestments was made from the same elaborate and luxurious materials that were used for the tabernacle's construction. And like the tabernacle's elaborate materials, exquisite furnishings, and beautiful tapestry, the priests' vestments worked to proclaim one important reality. Since sinful Israel could not draw near to God's presence in the tabernacle for fear of death, they needed a mediator. They needed someone to represent them before God and someone to be God's representative to them.

So God chose sinful Israelite men—Aaron and his sons—to represent all of sinful Israel. And God commanded that the high priest wear a breastplate with twelve embedded stones to represent the twelve tribes of Israel. The high priest and the priests were clothed in the same materials as the tabernacle and were sanctified so that they were covered in God's holiness. This way, when they entered the tabernacle, they would be protected from God's judgment of death upon sinners. When they stood before the people of Israel, they would reflect God and His holiness as they spoke His Word to them. The entire process of ordination, from the sanctification of the priests to the sanctification of their vestments, took seven days (see Ex 29:35).

On the eighth day (the beginning of the first day of the week), Aaron and the priests began their daily services of sacrifice. And with that, a new era for Israel began. Through the priests, God would ensure that His people had access to Him and that He could continue to dwell with them without them needing to fear death. With God in their midst, Israel could continue their journey from Sinai. They could travel to and inherit the Promised Land, just as God swore to Abraham, Isaac, and Jacob (see Lv 26:42). There, He would be their God, and they would be His people.

It took around eleven days for Israel to travel from Sinai to the edge of the Promised Land, specifically the hill country of the Ammonites: Kadesh-barnea (see Dt 1:2, 19). But when they arrived at the Promised Land, of which God told them to go in and take possession, Israel refused to obey the word of the Lord. They had sent out twelve spies, one from each tribe, to scout out the land for forty days. Ten of the twelve spies—all but Joshua and Caleb—advised the people not to go and take possession of the land, as God commanded, because "they are stronger than we are" (Nu 13:31). So rather than obeying God's command and confidently trusting in His promise to be with them and fight for them, as Joshua and Caleb assured them, faithless Israel despaired, wept, and refused to move an inch. Actions have consequences. Thanks to Moses' intercession once again, God pardoned Israel's sin, and they did not die. But they were forced to wander for forty years in the wilderness, one year for every day they spied out the land, until all those who had refused to fight and enter had died before they could enter the land God promised to them (see Nu 14:34).

During those forty years, Israel did what Israel did best. They grumbled against God and against His servants Moses and Aaron. At one point, when water was sparse, Israel again cried out, "Why have you brought the assembly of the LORD into this wilderness, that we should die here . . . ? And why have you made us come up out of Egypt to bring us to this evil place?" (Nu 20:4–5). Only this time, Moses was so sick and tired of their grumbling and rebellion that he failed to listen to God's command to speak to the rock at Meribah so that God could continue to show His holiness and faithful provision for His people. Instead, Moses and Aaron assembled all of Israel together, called them a bunch of rebels, and exasperatedly complained about how they must bring water out of the rock for Israel. Moses then struck the rock twice and left God out of the conversation altogether. And while God did provide water out of the rock for His people so that they may live, Moses and Aaron received a consequence for their sinful disobedience. God declared that Aaron and Moses would die before Israel entered the Promised Land.

This, however, was not the most severe judgment that Israel received for this sinful grumbling and rebellion against God during those forty years. While they were traveling around Edom, the land of Esau's descendants, Israel became impatient and grumbled against God and Moses once again. "Why have you brought us up out of Egypt to die in the wilderness? For there is no food and no water, and we loathe this worthless food" (Nu 21:5). When the Lord heard this, He sent poisonous serpents to bite the people so that many died. How many, you might wonder? Scripture never says. But the number was large enough to cause Israel to cry out in repentance: "We have sinned, for we have spoken against the LORD and against you" (Nu 21:7). And when the Lord saw their repentance and heard Moses' prayer on their behalf, He had compassion on them. He instructed Moses to make a bronze serpent, hang it on a pole, and lift it up. Then, when someone was bitten, they could look at it, trust in God's promise to save them, and live. It was through this cursed object hanging on a pole that God chose to save His people from the utter destruction of His judgment on their sin. By God's grace, Israel was spared. And by God's grace, after wandering in the wilderness for forty years, the Israelites arrived back at the land that was promised to them.

As Israel stood on the east bank of the Jordan river, on the plains of Moab overlooking the city of Jericho, Moses recounted to them the steadfast love of the Lord. He reminded them how God freed them from Egyptian slavery. He reminded them how God led them safely through the Red Sea with a mighty outstretched arm. He reminded them how the Lord provided for them in the wilderness for forty years by giving them food and drink and not even letting their clothes wear out. He reminded them of how the Lord faithfully led them to this rich and vibrant Promised Land, which He described with terms reminiscent of the Garden of Eden (see Dt 8:1–16; 11:1–12). He warned them to obey all the commandments and statutes that the Lord had given them so that they may live long in the land that God swore to give them. He told them to drive out the current inhabitants of the land, lest they become a snare to them and cause Israel to fall into worshiping their false gods and incur God's wrath, like they did in the wilderness with the fiery serpents. But what's more, Moses told them that in this land, God is going to "put His name and make His habitation" (Dt 12:5). God is going to continually dwell with His people in the land where they have permanent residence. Moses told them all of this, but he did not get to experience it firsthand. Like Aaron, Moses died before Israel entered the Promised Land. And for the next thirty days, Israel wept and mourned Moses' death.

Then, the Lord spoke to Joshua: "Just as I was with Moses, so I will be with you. I will not leave you or forsake you. Be strong and courageous, for you shall cause this people to inherit the land that I swore to their fathers to give them" (Jsh 1:5–6). But before Joshua set out for the Promised Land with Israel, he sent two spies to scout out Jericho. And while they were there, the spies encountered trouble when the king of Jericho learned of their presence. But God protected them. He used Rahab, a prostitute and Gentile (someone who is not from the nation of Israel) to hide these men from the king's search. Rahab, and all of Jericho for that matter, had heard of how God freed Israel from Egyptian slavery forty years earlier, dried up the Red Sea, and defeated all of Israel's enemies. And that terrified them. But unlike the rest of Jericho, Rahab believed that God had given Israel this land as He promised (see Jsh 2:9). God not only provided the Israelite spies with safe passage and protected them through the hand of Rahab but He also promised to save Rahab and her family from the great battle of Jericho.

I say *great battle* not because Israel fought bravely or because the battle between Israel and Jericho was fierce and long. I say the battle was great because the Lord of Sabaoth, the general of the heavenly armies, God Himself, appeared to and spoke with Joshua, telling him, like He told Moses, to "take off your sandals from your feet, for the place where you are standing is holy" (Jsh 5:15). The Lord then told Joshua how He was going to fight for His people yet again. For six days, Joshua was to take the Levitical priests with the ark of the covenant in hand, as well as the armed men of Israel positioned in front of and behind the ark, and march around the city one time while blowing seven rams horn trumpets continually. On the seventh day, they were to march around the city seven times, then victoriously blow the trumpets, and have all the people shout in victory. Then, God would reduce Jericho's fortified stone city wall to rubble, and Israel could enter the city and take possession of the land that God had promised to give them.

So Joshua and Israel did as the Lord commanded, and Jericho fell. Through the hands of Israel, God executed His judgment upon the faithless inhabitants of Jericho. For even though the current inhabitants of the Promised Land had heard about the one true God and His mighty deeds, they refused to believe in Him. Instead, they idolatrously worshiped false gods. And since the wages of sin is death, all the inhabitants of Jericho died that day. Only Rahab and her family, identified by a scarlet cord tied in her window, were spared and made part of the people of Israel.

While Jericho was the first great battle in the Promised Land, it would not be the last. In fact, it took twelve additional battles, including one where the Lord caused the sun to stand still in the sky, before Israel could inherit the Promised Land. Irrespective, battle after battle, the Lord fought for and through Israel. And battle after battle, Israel's possession of the Promised Land grew, from east to west, then south to north, until they had finally taken possession of the land the Lord swore to give to their forefathers: Abraham, Isaac, and Jacob.

Once the thirteen major battles had been won, Joshua divided the land into sections and gave each of the Israelite tribes a section of the Promised Land, except for the Levites, as they were to remain the stewards and priests of the tabernacle. Joshua then warned Israel not to sin by worshiping false gods—if they did, they would incur God's wrath. They, like Adam, would be kicked out of the Promised Land, out of God's presence. And though Israel responded by saying, "The LORD our God we will serve, and His voice we will obey," one seemingly insurmountable problem remained as they settled into the Promised Land (Jsh 24:24). God is perfect and holy, and they were still, by nature, sinful and unclean.

CHAPTER 4

PIECING IT TOGETHER: THE PROMISED LAND TO BABYLON AND BACK

As you might have guessed, things did not go well for Israel in the Promised Land. During Joshua's lifetime, Israel worshiped and served God. But when Joshua died, they began to do what is "evil in the sight of the LORD" (Jgs 2:11). Since the people of Israel had failed to drive out or devote the previous inhabitants of the Promised Land to destruction as the Lord had commanded them to do and as they had done in Jericho, the cohabitants became a snare to them (see Jgs 1:1–31). Their intermarriages with the Canaanites, Hittites, Amorites, Perizzites, Hivites, Jebusites, and Philistines caused all kinds of problems for them. Because they had yoked themselves to the idolatrous, unbelieving descendants of Noah's son Ham, the Israelites forgot about God.[20] They failed to catechize or teach their children about who God is and what He had done for them. This in turn led to their participation in and adoption of pagan worship practices. In fact, over the next three hundred years, Israel fell into a vicious cycle of idolatry (see Jgs 2:16–19). And this vicious cycle followed a tragic, yet predictable pattern.

They would abandon God and worship the gods of the people who were around them. If a particular Israelite tribe lived among the Canaanites, Hittites, Amorites, Perizzites, Hivites, or Jebusites, then they would "whore" after Baal and Ashtaroth.[21] This meant that they would engage in sexual intercourse with cult prostitutes at the designated high places of worship in hopes that when Baal and Astaroth saw them, they, too, would engage in sexual intercourse with each other, which would result in fertile rain for the people's crops.[22] If the tribe lived among the Philistines, then they would offer sacrifices to Dagon, another agricultural fertility god. Regardless of which false god Israel worshiped, they incurred God's wrath. God would then execute His judgment upon faithless Israel through the hand of the cohabiting enemy nation which would plunder and oppress them. When the Israelites could no longer endure the enemy oppression, they would cry out to God in repentance. God would raise up a judge, or military deliver, from one of Israel's tribes, and the judge would save them. And when the judge died, Israel would return to their vomitous sin, wallow in idolatry, and become even more corrupt than before (see Jgs 2:19).

This vicious cycle occurred twelve times. And twelve times the Lord

---

20 For a full list of Ham's descendants, see Gn 10:6–20.

21 Jgs 2:17; 8:27, 33; *Ashtaroth* is also known as Asherah and Ashtoreth.

22 R. Reed Lessing and Andrew E. Steinmann, *Prepare the Way of the Lord: An Introduction to the Old Testament* (St. Louis: Concordia Publishing House, 2014), 169.

raised up a judge to free Israel from their oppressors. Othniel victoriously battled the king of Mesopotamia. Left-handed Ehud plunged his small double-edged sword so far into the morbidly obese king of Moab's belly that it got encapsulated and concealed by his fat and dung came out of him. Shamgar slew six hundred Philistines with an oxgoad (essentially a staff with a metal point on the end for urging oxen along or clearing mud off a plow). Deborah urged her petrified military commander Barak to fight against the Canaanites, accompanied him on his journey, and spoke of how a woman named Jael would deliver the final battle blow by driving a tent peg through the Canaanite general's head with a hammer. Gideon and his three hundred men slaughtered 120,000 Midianites in battle. Jephthah was victorious over the Moabite army. Tola, Jair, Ibzan, Elon, and Abdon led Israel and ensured military peace. Samson slew one thousand Philistines with a donkey's jawbone, and he collapsed a temple of Dagon on himself and three thousand Philistines by toppling the central support pillars with his bare hands.

While these judges delivered Israel from the hand of its enemy, they did not tackle the real problem. Sin still lurks in the heart of man. Idolatry, sexual immorality, theft, murder, adultery, slander, coveting, deceit, and wickedness still abound. This is why God was confined to a tent, veiled behind a curtain, and only beheld by the high priest once a year. This is why when all of the judges died and there was no leader, no king in Israel, "everyone did what was right in his own eyes" (Jgs 21:25). Israel needs more than a judge, more than a tribal deliverer, even more than an ordinary king. They need a savior, one who will crush the head of the serpent and restore to them the unveiled presence of God.

It is no wonder that during the chaotic time of the judges, we receive a particular piece of the puzzle that focuses on a little family from Bethlehem in Judah. Elimelech, his wife Naomi, and his two sons, Mahlon and Chilion, sojourn to Moab because of a great famine. Over the course of ten years, this family experiences a great deal of sorrows and joys. Elimelech dies. Mahlon and Chilion each marry a Moabite woman. But not long after marrying Orpah and Ruth, both sons die. Grieving Naomi, who feels like the Lord's hand is against her, urges her two widowed daughters-in-law to return to their Moabite families. Orpah does, but Ruth chooses to stay with Naomi and travel to Bethlehem. In Bethlehem, Naomi and Ruth are in danger of losing their house and land, since Elimelech has died. Boaz, a relative of Naomi's, has compassion on them and redeemed, or "bought back," their land for them by marrying Ruth. But what's more, the Lord blessed this marital union of Boaz and Ruth with a child, named Obed. Obed was the father of Jesse. Jesse was the father of David. And David was no ordinary king.

After the first king of Israel, Saul, had rejected God's Word by refusing to execute His judgment of death upon the faithless nation of Amalek (see 1Sm 15:1–34), David was chosen by God to be king of Israel (see 1Sm 16:1–13). God's choice was surprising even to the Lord's prophet Samuel. He expected that the Lord would choose the firstborn son, but God reversed the order. He made the last first and the first last. God told Samuel to anoint David, the youngest of Jesse's eight sons, with the horn of oil that he may become king of Israel. For contrary to what Samuel thought, the Lord does not look at outward appearances. He looks at the heart (see 1Sm 16:7). And David was a man after God's own heart (see 1Sm 13:14; Ac 13:22). In fact, upon his anointing, the Spirit of the Lord rushed upon David, and God was with him.

In the Spirit of the Lord, David slew the Philistine giant Goliath, knocking him to the ground with a slinged stone and cutting off Goliath's head with his own sword. In the Spirit of the Lord, David refused to kill Saul, recognizing that he was still "the LORD's anointed" (1Sm 24:6). In the Spirit of the Lord, David became a wise and brave king of Israel who conquered many enemy nations, established a capital city in Jerusalem, brought the ark safely there, and even wanted to build God a more permanent structure than the tent where it currently resided. God even promised David that his kingdom would be established forever (see 2Sm 7:16). In many respects, David looked like the fulfillment of everything that God had promised to Abraham and Sarah when He said, "Kings of people shall come from you," and to Judah when He said, "The scepter shall not depart from Judah, nor the ruler's staff from between his feet" (Gn 17:16; 49:10; see also Gn 17:6). He looked like the fulfillment of the promise in every way, except one. David was a sinner.

This is made abundantly clear when late one spring afternoon, while strolling on his palace roof, David sees a beautiful woman bathing. He covetously inquires who she is. And after finding out that this woman, named Bathsheba, is married to his loyal soldier Uriah the Hittite, David takes her. He commits adultery with her. He impregnates her. And then he devises a fiendish plot to try to make it look like Uriah's child. But when that fails, David has Uriah killed in battle so that he can take Bathsheba as his wife and cover up his sins.

While Israel is fooled, God is not. The Lord sent His prophet Nathan to confront David in his sin, saying, "Why have you despised the word of the Lord, to do what is evil in His sight? You have struck down Uriah the Hittite with the sword [of the Ammonites] and have taken his wife to be your wife" (2Sm 12:9). When David heard this, he repentantly cried, "I have sinned against the Lord" (2Sm 12:13). He even begged God to

> Create in me a clean heart, O God,
>
> and renew a right spirit within me.
>
> Cast me not away from Your presence,
>
> and take not Your Holy Spirit from me.
>
> Restore to me the joy of Your salvation,
>
> and uphold me with a willing spirit. (Ps 51:10–12)

And God did. He forgave David. He took away David's sin and allowed the Holy Spirit to remain with him. But David's sins also carried earthly consequences. David and Bathsheba's child died. One of his sons, Absalom, rebelled against him and tried to take his kingship from him. Moreover, since David had shed a lot of blood, he was forbidden from building a more permanent structure for God's dwelling.

Yet even though David had failed God, God did not fail David. Not only did the Lord grant repentance, faith, forgiveness, and long life to David. He also granted David, through Bathsheba, another son, Solomon, to take his throne. And while there are many notable things about Solomon, who took the throne as "a little child" (1Ki 3:7) and was granted a wise and discerning heart by God, the pinnacle of his forty-year reign was the building and dedication of the temple. In truth, this honor and achievement was bestowed upon Solomon even before he became king. Right before David died, he gave Solomon the blueprints he had drawn up for the temple and told him, "The Lord has chosen you to build a house for the sanctuary; be strong and do it" (1Ch 28:10). Additionally, God promised Solomon, "If you walk in My statutes and obey My rules and keep all My commandments and walk in them, then I will establish My word with you, which I spoke to David your father. And I will dwell among the children of Israel and will not forsake My people Israel" (1Ki 6:12–13).

So Solomon built the temple according to the specifications given to him, with a few additions. In many respects, the temple resembled the tabernacle. It was still divided into three distinct sections: the Most Holy Place, the Holy Place, and the courtyard. It was constructed from many of the same elaborate building materials: gold, silver, bronze, blue yarn, purple yarn, scarlet yarn, fine linens, and precious gems. It even still housed the table for the bread of the Presence, a lampstand, the altar of incense, the altar of burnt offering, and the finely woven angelic cherubim tapestries embroidered on the veil, which still separated the Most Holy Place from the Holy Place. And like the tabernacle, all of the temple's elaborate materials, exquisite furnishings, and beautiful tapestry worked to proclaim this one important reality: God now dwells with His people!

The temple, however, had some significant differences from the tabernacle. First, instead of acacia wood, the temple was constructed with the mighty cedars of Lebanon and the finest of cypress wood. Second, instead of curtains for outer walls, it had the choicest quarried and hewn stone. Third, instead of curtains with embroidered cherubim for inner walls, it is made of cedar, with cherubim, palm trees, and flowers carved into it, and then overlaid with pure gold. The floor also was made of cedar and overlaid with gold. Finally, the temple was double the length and triple the height of the tabernacle (see 1Ki 6:2–10; 2Ch 3:3–4). Instead of being roughly forty-five feet long and fifteen feet wide, it was about ninety feet long and thirty feet wide. Instead of being fifteen feet high, it was forty-five feet high. Thus, instead of one lampstand, there were ten lampstands. The size of the special curtain or veil, which divided the Holy Place and the Most Holy Place, was also increased so that it stretched the full width and height of the inner temple. These significant differences, like the similarities, also worked to proclaim one important reality: permanence!

If the tabernacle proclaimed the reality that "God now dwells with His people," the temple proclaimed the reality that "God now more permanently dwells with His people." Hence, upon its completion and dedication, Solomon declared to God in the midst of the assembly of the congregation of Israel, "I have indeed built You an exalted house, a place for You to dwell in forever" (1Ki 8:13). And as the assembly of Israel watched the priests and Levites bring the holy vessels and the ark of the covenant out of the tabernacle to place them into the temple, the divine cloud of God's presence filled the newly dedicated temple just like it did at the dedication of the tabernacle.

Yet despite the fanfare, pomp, and circumstance of Solomon's majestic festival, which was to mark a new era for Israel of inestimable and unfathomable joy in God's permanent presence, the day rang solemnly hollow. Solemn because at the climax of King Solomon's dedication prayer, the words "for there is no one who does not sin" (1Ki 8:46) filled the air with the sourest of notes, reminding all of Israel that they are sinful and unclean. Hollow because when the divine cloud fills the temple, not even the priests can remain. They are temporarily forced to exit on account of God's holy presence. And while God verbally acknowledges that He has heard their prayer, consecrated the temple, and placed His name there forever, He also admonishes them to walk with Him as David walked, to obey His commandments and worship Him alone, lest He cast them out of His presence and make this house they have built for Him a "heap of ruins" (1Ki 9:4–9).

As harsh as those words sound, the reality was much worse. Solomon ignored the word of the Lord concerning intermarriages with the other nations. He did what was evil in God's sight. He practiced idolatry. His seven hundred wives and three hundred concubines turned his heart away from the one true God and toward false gods: Ashtoreth and Milcom. Consequently, God chastised Solomon, saying, "I will surely tear the kingdom from you and will give it to your servant. Yet for the sake of David your father I will not do it in your days, but I will tear it out of the hand of your son" (1Ki 11:11–12).

And He did. God is faithful to His Word. When Solomon's son Rehoboam took the throne, the kingdom of Israel was torn in two. Rather than having mercy upon, caring for, and serving all the assembly of Israel as a king should, Rehoboam sinned. He ignored Israel's plea to "lighten the hard service of your father and his heavy yoke on us" (1Ki 12:4). He ignored the advice of the elders to love and serve the people. He listened to the advice of his young friends. He arrogantly, pridefully, and harshly retorted, "Whereas my father laid on you a heavy yoke, I will add to your yoke. My father disciplined you with whips, but I will discipline you with scorpions" (1 Ki 12:11). And with that, Israel is ripped apart. The tribes of Asher, Dan, Ephraim, Gad, Issachar, Manasseh, Naphtali, Reuben, Simeon, and Zebulun rebel and form a new nation: the Kingdom of Israel or the Northern Kingdom. The remaining two tribes, Judah and Benjamin, establish the Kingdom of Judah or the Southern Kingdom.

Shortly after their rebellion, the Northern Kingdom, Israel, made Jeroboam, son of Nebat, their first king. This was in accordance with the word of the Lord as spoken to Jeroboam by the prophet Ahijah during Solomon's reign and apostasy. But what was not in accordance with the word of the Lord was Jeroboam's idolatry. He feared that if the people regularly traveled to Jerusalem in the Southern Kingdom to offer sacrifices to the Lord in the temple, "then the heart of this people will turn again to their lord, to Rehoboam king of Judah, and they will kill me and return to Rehoboam king of Judah" (1Ki 12:27). To prevent this and safeguard the people's loyalty, Jeroboam constructed two golden calves. He placed one at the top of the Northern Kingdom, in the city of Dan. The other he placed at the bottom of the Northern Kingdom, in the city of Bethel, where Jacob had the peculiar dream about angels ascending and descending on a ladder. Additionally, he built two temples around the calves, ordained non-Levitical priests to offer sacrifices to them, and piously proclaimed to all of Israel, "You have gone up to Jerusalem long enough. Behold your gods, O Israel, who brought you up out of the land of Egypt" (1 Ki 12:28).

The idolatrous sins of Jeroboam are not only detestable in God's sight but also a defining characteristic of all subsequent kings of Israel, as shown in Figure 2. Every king of Israel does what is evil in the sight of the Lord. Like their stubborn, stiff-necked, hard-hearted ancestors, they ignored God's laws and commandments. They exchanged the worship of the one true God for the worship of whatever god was prominent among the fellow inhabitants of the land. They practiced divination as they worshiped the sun, moon, and stars. They offered sacrifices to Chemosh and Molech by burning their children alive on their altars. They even frequently engaged in sexual intercourse with cult prostitutes in worship of Baal and Asherah. Whatever the god, the kings of Israel and their subjects whored after it.

KINGS OF ISRAEL (The Northern Kingdom)

NAME:	JUDGMENT OF GOD
Jeroboam (1Ki 12:20–14:20)	Did evil
Nadab (1Ki 15:25–32)	Did evil
Baasha (1Ki 15:33–16:7)	Did evil
Elah (1Ki 16:8–14)	Did evil
Zimri (1Ki 16:15–20)	Did evil
Omri (1Ki 16:21–28)	Did evil
Ahab (1Ki 16:29–22:40)	Did evil
Ahaziah (2Ki 1:1–17)	Did evil
Jehoram (2Ki 3:1–3)	Did evil
Jehu (2Ki 9:30–10:36)	Did evil
Jehoahaz (2Ki 13:1–9)	Did evil
Jehoash (2Ki 13:10–25)	Did evil
Jeroboam II (2Ki 14:23–29)	Did evil
Zechariah (2Ki 15:8–12)	Did evil
Shallum (2Ki 15:13–16)	Did evil
Menahem (2Ki 15:17–22)	Did evil
Pekahiah (2Ki 15:23–26)	Did evil
Pekah (2Ki 15:27–31)	Did evil
Hoshea (2Ki 17)	Did evil

Figure 2: Kings of Israel

Through it all, the Lord was patient, just like in the days of Noah. He did not desire the death of a sinner. He wanted Israel to repent and live with Him. That is why He sent them the prophet Elijah, who challenged Ahab and Jezebel's 450 Baal prophets to a sacrificial competition, saying, "You call upon the name of your god, and I will call upon the name of the LORD, and the God who answers by fire, He is God" (1 Ki 18:24). Elijah made a mockery of Baal and his prophets, first by sarcastically accusing Baal of not answering because he might be deep in thought or even using the bathroom, and then by praying to the God of Abraham, Isaac, and Jacob, who sent down fire, which consumed Elijah's burnt offering, altar, stones, and the dust that surrounded it. Still, Israel did not fully repent. Overall, their hearts remained as hard as stone.

So the Lord sent the prophet Elisha, who received a double portion of Elijah's spirit after watching him being taken to heaven in a whirlwind. He raised the Shunammite woman's dead son, healed Naaman of leprosy by God's word to wash in the Jordan, and prophesied of a seven-year famine due to Israel's idolatrous sin. The Lord also sent the prophets Hosea and Amos to plead with Israel to "return to the LORD" (Hos 6:1) or He "will send you into exile beyond Damascus" (Am 5:27). During this time, the Lord even sent the prophet Jonah, via three days and three nights in the belly of a great fish, to the Gentile enemy nation of Assyria to preach repentance and faith to the inhabitants of their capital city, Nineveh.

Yet despite God's incessant pleas through the mouths of His prophets, the Israelites, unlike the Ninevites, refused to repent. They "walked in all the sins that Jeroboam did. They did not depart from them, until the Lord removed Israel out of His sight" (2Ki 17:22–23). And in 722 BC, God allowed the enemy nation of Assyria to march into the Northern Kingdom, destroy it, and take Israel captive into exile and slavery.

The Southern Kingdom of Judah was slightly more faithful with respect to the worship of the one true God, as seen in Figure 3. Despite the hatred and numerous civil wars with Israel, Judah had a total of nine kings who did what was right in the eyes of the Lord.

Asa, Jehoshaphat, Joash, Amaziah, Uzziah, and Jotham all worshiped the God of Abraham, Isaac, and Jacob, who brought His people out of slavery in the land of Egypt. Moreover, these kings sought to remove the despicable cult prostitution of Baal and Asherah, as well as their idolatrous statues, even though many of the inhabitants of Judah continued to offer sacrifices to these gods. And unlike their predecessors, Hezekiah and Josiah even managed to destroy Baal and Asherah's idolatrous temples and altars.

It can also be said of Hezekiah that in the face of a terminal illness and the threat of an Assyrian invasion, he clung to the Lord fervently in prayer. Subsequently, the Lord heard his prayer. He added fifteen years to Hezekiah's life and saved Judah from Assyrian destruction and captivity (see 2Ki 20:5–7).

KINGS OF JUDAH (The Southern Kingdom)

NAME:	JUDGMENT OF GOD
Rehoboam (1Ki 11:42–14:31)	Did evil
Abijam (1Ki 14:31–15:8)	Did evil
Asa (1Ki 15:8–24)	Did right
Jehoshaphat (1Ki 22:41–50)	Did right
Jehoram (2Ki 8:16–23)	Did evil
Ahaziah (2Ki 8:24–9:29)	Did evil
Athaliah (2Ki 11)	Did evil
Joash (2Ki 12)	Did right
Amaziah (2Ki 14:1–22)	Did right
Uzziah (2Ki 15:1–7)	Did right
Jotham (2Ki 15:32–38)	Did right
Ahaz (2Ki 16)	Did evil
Hezekiah (2Ki 18–20)	Did right
Manasseh (2Ki 21:1–18)	Did evil
Amon (2Ki 21:19–26)	Did evil
Josiah (2Ki 22:1–23:30)	Did right
Jehoahaz (2Ki 23:31–33)	Did evil
Jehoiakim (2Ki 23:34–24:5)	Did evil
Jehoiachin (2Ki 24:6–16)	Did evil
Zedekiah (2Ki 24:17–25:30)	Did evil

Figure 3: Kings of Judah

During Josiah's reign, the Book of the Law, the Word of God, was discovered by the high priest Hilkiah. It was then read to Josiah, who tore his clothes in repentance and set out to reform Judah. He repaired the damaged and sorely neglected temple, burned the statues of Asherah that had been placed in the temple, destroyed all the idolatrous worship areas that had been erected in Judah. Then he offered sacrifices to God there, publicly read the Book of the Law to the people of Judah, and made a covenant with God that he and all of Judah would stop their idolatry. Josiah even went so far as to march into the former Northern Kingdom of Israel where he then tore down and burned the "altar at Bethel, the high place erected by Jeroboam the son of Nebat" (2Ki 23:15).

Regardless of all of Josiah's reforms, "Judah also did not keep the commandments of the LORD their God, but walked in the customs that Israel had introduced" (2Ki 17:19). Thus, the other rulers, including Queen Athaliah, did what was evil in the Lord's sight. They, too, whored after other gods, burning their children alive on the altars of Chemosh and Molech, practicing divination, and engaging in sexual intercourse with the cult prostitutes of Baal and Asherah. And despite the myriad warnings from the Lord's prophets—Obadiah, Joel, Isaiah, Micah, Nahum, Jeremiah, Zephaniah, Ezekiel, and Habakkuk—the Southern Kingdom persisted in their hard-heartedness and refused to repent. So, just like Adam and Eve in the garden and Israel to the north, God casts Judah "out from His [presence]" (2 Ki 24:20).

In 586 BC, King Nebuchadnezzar and his Babylonian army marched into Jerusalem. And climactically, right before this momentous event, the Lord, who has been dwelling in the temple enthroned between the cherubim on the ark in the glory cloud, departs (see Ezk 10). Jerusalem and the temple are then ransacked and razed. And the Southern Kingdom of Judah is taken captive into Babylonian exile and slavery.

Because of sin, Israel and Judah, which stood so proud, tall, and victorious with God in its midst, now looks like a cut-down, defeated, dried-up, withered tree stump. Because of sin, Israel and Judah, which were so vibrant and full of life from God's presence, now look like a desolate valley of filthy, decayed, dried-up, lifeless bones. By the waters of Babylon, the exiles weep and mourn, wondering whether life can come from a withered tree stump or if lifeless bones can live (see Ezk 37:11). They were wondering if they would ever return from exile and rebuild Jerusalem and the temple. To them, it all seemed so hopeless as they cried, "The LORD has forsaken me; my Lord has forgotten me" (Is 49:14).

But like a mother cannot forget her nursing child, neither can the Lord forget His people and the promise He made to them. That is why, even before exile, He spoke through the mouth of His prophets, saying, "There shall come forth a shoot from the stump of Jesse, and a branch from his roots shall bear fruit" (Is 11:1). Because "the virgin shall conceive and bear a son, and shall call His name Immanuel" (Is 7:14). That is, a child would be born, a son would be given (see Is 9:6). He would come from Bethlehem Ephrathah (see Mi 5:2). He would grow up like a tender shoot to have the iniquity of all laid upon Him, that He might be pierced for our transgressions and crushed for our iniquities (see Is 53:2–6). In this way, the Lord would once again be in the midst of His people (see Zep 3:17). In this way, the Lord would once again breathe life into lifeless bones, raising them from their graves, putting His Spirit in them so that they may live, and once again bring them into their own land (see Ezk 37:9–14). And on that day, the "ransomed of the LORD shall return and come to Zion with singing; everlasting joy shall be upon their heads; they shall obtain gladness and joy, and sorrow and sighing shall flee away" (Is 35:10). In short, God would send a Promised Child who would crush the head of the serpent and restore to them the Promised Land, the very presence of God.

Until that restoration, even during exile, even in Babylon, the Lord would not forget about or abandon His people, the faithful remnant. Hence when Shadrach, Meshach, and Abednego were thrown into a burning fiery furnace for refusing to bow down and worship the ninety-foot golden statue that Nebuchadnezzar had built, God protected them. He provided a fourth man, whose appearance was like "a son of the gods" (Dn 3:25), to save them to the degree that when they emerged, their clothes were unburned, their hair unsinged, and they didn't even smell of smoke (see Dn 3:27). This in turn caused the Gentile King Nebuchadnezzar to exclaim, "Blessed be the God of Shadrach, Meshach, and Abednego, who has sent His angel and delivered His servants, who trusted in Him, and set aside the king's command, and yielded up their bodies rather than serve and worship any god except their own God" (Dn 3:28). And when the prophet Daniel was thrown into a lions' den for praying to God three times a day, the Lord protected His servant by shutting the lions' mouths that he might emerge unharmed (see Dn 6). Not only did God protect His people during their time of exile but He also delivered them from it.

After seventy long years, God sent a deliverer, Cyrus, king of Persia, to conquer the Babylonians, free Judah from captivity, and allow them to return to Jerusalem to rebuild the city and the temple (see 2Ch 36:22–23; Ezr 1:1–11). And they did. Judah returned and rebuilt both Jerusalem and the temple. Sadly and tragically, however, God's presence did not return to fill it. That is why the prophet Haggai proclaimed, "Who is left among you who saw this house in its former glory? How do you see it now? Is it not as nothing in your eyes?" (Hg 2:3). It is also why the priests, Levites, and elders who had seen and participated in the first temple wept at the dedication of the second temple (see Ezr 3:12). God no longer physically dwelt with His people. Just like in the Garden of Eden, sin had driven out God's presence from among His people.

For the next four hundred years through the end of the Old Testament, there was no prophet in all the land. God was silent—deafeningly silent. And the people of God, like Adam and Eve before them, were waiting, watching, and wondering, "Where are You, God?" Where is the Promised Child who will crush the head of the serpent and restore to us the presence of God?

CHAPTER 5

HELD TOGETHER BY CHRIST

Into this silence, after four hundred years, God speaks. He first speaks to a priest named Zechariah, who was burning incense on the altar of incense in the temple. The angel Gabriel appeared on the right side of the altar with a message for Zechariah and his barren wife, Elizabeth. "Your prayer has been heard, and your wife Elizabeth will bear you a son . . . he will be filled with the Holy Spirit . . . he will turn many of the children of Israel to the Lord their God" (Lk 1:13–16). At first, Zechariah rejects the word of the Lord. Consequently, he is made unable to speak about what he had seen and heard in the temple. However, upon his son's birth, Zechariah etches the name that Gabriel had given him into a writing tablet. "His name is John" (Lk 1:63). And with that, his tongue is loosed, and he eagerly proclaims what was spoken to him. All who hear it wonder if this is the Promised Child.

John, however, was not the Promised Child. It is true that as he grew up, he became strong in spirit, the hand of the Lord was upon him, and the word of God even came to him (see Lk 1:80; 3:2). It is true that he preached, saying, "Repent, for the kingdom of heaven is at hand" (Mt 3:2), and he baptized for the forgiveness of sins, as Isaiah foretold. But all of this was to "prepare the way of the Lord" (Lk 3:4–6). All of this was to turn Israel and Judah from their idolatrous ways so that they may look and long for the Promised Child to advent or "come" among us. Hence when asked by the priests and Levites, John readily and wholeheartedly confessed, "I am not the Christ [meaning the Anointed One]" (Jn 1:20).

So God speaks again. Only six months after God spoke to Zechariah and Elizabeth became pregnant, the angel Gabriel appeared to a virgin named Mary. The words Gabriel annunciated are both simple and complex. Simple because a woman can conceive and give birth to a son. It happens all the time. It's been happening since Adam first knew his wife, Eve, and she gave birth to a son. Complex because Mary is a lowly virgin. Complex because the child will be called "holy—the Son of God" (Lk 1:35) who sits on King David's throne and reigns over "the house of Jacob" (Lk 1:33)— meaning all twelve tribes, both Israel and Judah—forever. Yet Gabriel assures Mary that the Mighty One, God Himself, is about to do a great thing. "The Holy Spirit will come upon you, and the power of the Most High will overshadow you" (Lk 1:35). Unlike Zechariah, Mary believes the word Gabriel spoke to her. She faithfully exclaims, "Behold, I am the servant of the Lord; let it be to me according to your word" (Lk 1:38).

When the angel departs, Mary immediately travels to see her relative Elizabeth. For Gabriel also mentioned to Mary that Elizabeth, who was once barren, is now six months pregnant. Remarkably, as Mary arrives and greets Elizabeth, baby John begins to leap for joy in Elizabeth's uterus. And at the same time, Elizabeth proclaims, "Blessed are you among women, and blessed is the fruit of your womb! And why is this granted to me that the mother of my Lord should come to me?" (Lk 1:42–43). But just why is John jumping for joy? And how does Elizabeth know that Mary is pregnant with not just any baby but the "Lord"? It is not like Mary has a pregnancy belly or baby bump yet. Again, when Gabriel appears to Mary, Elizabeth was already six months pregnant. Mary then quickly goes to see Elizabeth and stays with her for three months until Elizabeth gives birth to John. Accordingly, Elizabeth cannot know by sight. She knows because she was filled with the Holy Spirit (see Lk 1:41).

The Holy Spirit is also the cause of great joy for Mary in this moment. For in the Spirit-filled words of joyous Elizabeth, Mary knows for certain that the prophet Isaiah's words are being fulfilled. The virgin has conceived a son. And not just any son—Elizabeth's Lord. John's Lord. Mary's Lord. The Lord! Miraculously and majestically, God takes the lowly and humble womb of the virgin Mary and crowns it with glory and honor by filling it with the Son of God. Astonishingly, God chose Mary, who in the eyes of the world was nothing, and made her the *Theotokos*,[23] "the mother of God."[24] This is the cause of Mary's song of praise, the Magnificat, in which her soul magnifies the Lord and her spirit rejoices in God, her Savior (see Lk 1:46–47). Because through her, God is fulfilling His promise spoken throughout the Old Testament.

This miraculous, majestic, and astonishing work of God is a source of great comfort and joy for Joseph, Mary's husband, as well. After Mary had returned from visiting Elizabeth, Joseph heartbreakingly discovered that she was "with child" (Mt 1:18). Rather than publicly stoning her to death for her apparent adultery as the Law permits,[25] Joseph mercifully decided to "divorce her quietly" (Mt 1:19) so that she may live. Regardless, Joseph

---

23 Pronounced thee-uh-TOE-kose. The literal translation of the word means "God-bearer."

24 FC SD VIII 24.

25 See Dt 22:13–29.

is dismayed. Yet in the midst of Joseph's consternation, an angel of God appears to him in a dream and reveals that Mary is not an adulterer. Her child is from the Holy Spirit. They are to name Him Jesus, because He will save His people from the very thing that has separated them from their holy and perfect God since Adam and Eve's fall into sin. "He will save His people from their sins" (Mt 1:21). Essentially, the angel tells Joseph that finally, at long last, God has fulfilled His Old Testament promise of divine presence. Here, in the womb of Mary, is the Promised Child, Jesus, who has come to crush the serpent and restore to us the presence of God.

Figure 4: The Promised Seed

That reality is precisely why the New Testament, with Matthew's Gospel, begins with the words, "The book of the genealogy of Jesus Christ, the son of David, the son of Abraham" (Mt 1:1). Through a genealogical list of names grouped into three sets of fourteen, or six sets of seven, Matthew not only recounts the history of Israel but also reveals that Jesus is the climax and culmination of that history. Put differently, "the fullness of time" (Gal 4:4) has come and God is sending forth His own Son, Jesus, to fulfill the promise spoken to David and Abraham.

Similarly, Luke's Gospel also includes a genealogical list of names, which incorporates David and Abraham but spans all the way back through the genealogies of Genesis 10 and Genesis 5. Luke traces Jesus' lineage through Seth to Adam. In doing so, he reveals that Jesus is the fulfillment of the promise of divine presence, which was spoken to very familiar Old Testament patriarchs: David,

Jesse, Obed, Boaz, Judah, Jacob, Isaac, Abraham, Peleg, Shem, Noah, Seth, and Adam. What's more, by saying Jesus is "the son of Adam, the son of God" (Lk 3:38), Luke declares that someone greater than Adam, a new Adam, a second Adam, has come (see 1Co 15:21–22, 45). His name is Jesus, and in Him both Adam and God are inseparably joined together as one. Put more simply, Jesus is both God and man.

Jesus' two natures are evident by the fact that Jesus was conceived by the Holy Spirit in Mary's womb. However, it is made more abundantly clear in the Gospels' birth narratives. For instance, in Matthew's Gospel, after the angel tells Joseph to take Mary as his wife and name the baby inside of her Jesus, Matthew then quotes Isaiah 7:14: "Behold, the virgin shall conceive and bear a son, and they shall call His name Immanuel." He then adds the appositive phrase, "which means, God with us" (Mt 1:23), to Isaiah's prophecy to make sure that Joseph knows the profundity of the title *Immanuel*. Veiled in the human flesh of this living, leaping lineage of David is none other than God Himself, who has come to save His people from their sin.

Luke's narrative of Jesus' birth, which is the most detailed, is less overt with respect to Jesus' two natures, God and man. However, it is no less majestic. For Luke, the majesty is hidden in ordinary yet breathtakingly beautiful details. He speaks about ordinary commonplace events and experiences: a Roman emperor named Caesar Augustus, a governor of Syria named Quirinius, a census, a city called Bethlehem, a genealogy or lineage of David, a husband and wife, a pregnancy, the birth of a son, shepherds, and flocks of sheep. Through these ordinary details, Luke declares that this historical event is as familiar to us as our daily lives, human in every way.

At the same time, these ordinary details are reported in an extraordinary way. While Mary is giving birth to her firstborn son, wrapping Him in swaddling cloths, and laying Him in a feeding trough, heaven is breaking forth in exuberant joy. To shepherds who were caring for their sheep in the same area that David once had, an angel appears and speaks of joyous good news for everyone. Today, a Savior was born in Bethlehem, the city of David. He is "Christ the Lord" (Lk 2:11). And with that announcement, a plethora of heavenly host appear and sing to God a hymn of praise, the Gloria in Excelsis or "Glory to God in the highest, and on earth peace among those with whom He is pleased" (Lk 2:14). In these breathtakingly beautiful details, Luke reveals that this baby is not only ordinary but extraordinary. "For in Him the whole fullness of deity [God] dwells bodily" (Col 2:9). Consequently, in the flesh of this infant, heaven and earth, God and man, are no longer at enmity. They are at peace. They are reconciled, for He has come as their Savior.

The Gospel of John's narrative of Jesus' birth is brief but comprehensive. When John speaks of Jesus' birth, he begins by recounting the words of creation in Genesis 1:1: "In the beginning." Interestingly, John does not start the narrative with the act of God speaking creation into existence. He starts by talking about what existed eternally before creation, "the Word" (Jn 1:1). John speaks about both the distinctiveness of "the Word," who "was with God," as well as the unity of "the Word," who "was God" (Jn 1:1). He declares that the world and everything in it was created through the Word (see Jn 1:3). But what's more, John proclaims that "the Word became flesh and dwelt among us, and we have seen His glory, glory as of the only Son from the Father, full of grace and truth" (Jn 1:14). With these brief words, John announces that the Creator physically entered into His creation. The eternal Word, the only Son of God the Father, became flesh. God is actually incarnate. He shares in our flesh and blood (see Heb 2:14). He dwells with us!

John reiterates and expounds on the significance of this reality when Jesus, over thirty years later (see Lk 3:23), enters the temple, scatters the money-changers' coins, overturns their tables, and drives the sellers of sacrificial animals out of the temple with a handmade whip of cords. When Jesus is asked to prove, with a sign, the authority by which He entered the temple and did these things, He replies, "Destroy this temple, and in three days I will raise it!" (Jn 2:19). The Jews who hear this statement think that Jesus is referring to the second temple, which was rebuilt over a period of twenty years after Babylonian exile, and which Herod remodeled during his reign. But John notes that the temple to which Jesus refers is His own body (see Jn 2:21). John wants everyone to know and believe for certain that the flesh of Jesus is the new temple, which is greater than the former (see Hg 2:9) because now the presence of God is not confined to a building, veiled behind a curtain, beheld by a priest only once a year, but rather, it is out in the open, veiled in flesh, and is to be beheld by all people.

1 Kings 6:12-13   John 2:19

THE PRESENCE OF GOD

Figure 5: The Presence of God

Now, given the two natures of Christ—Jesus being both true God and true man, as seen in His birth narratives—you might wonder what He was like as a child. You might wonder what His favorite food was? What games He liked to play? How He spent His free time? Or thousands of other normal, ordinary questions you would ask a child. But the truth is, we really don't have answers to a lot of the questions we want to ask. That's because there are only four stories of Jesus' childhood in Scripture. And while four stories don't answer all the questions, they certainly tell us exactly what we need to know about Jesus' childhood.

The first story we are given occurs when Jesus is eight days old. Luke records that at the end of that day, "He was circumcised" and "called Jesus" (Lk 2:21). Though short, this one verse tells us two vital aspects of Jesus' early infancy. First, Jesus' circumcision on the eighth day reveals that He kept the covenant of circumcision that God gave to Abraham back in Genesis 17:9–11, when God renamed Abram to Abraham and reminded him that the Promised Child would come from him and be a blessing for all nations. Second, with the name *Jesus*, the angel's words to Mary and Joseph are fulfilled. Their infant son is now publicly declared to be and known as the One who saves His people from their sins.

The second story of Jesus' childhood occurs when He is about forty days old. With their infant son in their arms, Mary and Joseph travel to the temple in Jerusalem. Why? Because Mary needed to be purified from the ceremonial uncleanness she incurred by giving birth (see Lv 12:1–8). And Jesus, as Mary's firstborn son, needed to be consecrated, or presented, to the Lord (see Ex 13:2, 12). In other words, both needed to do what God's Law required of them. This is so crucial that in the nineteen verses it takes for Luke to tell the story of Jesus' presentation, he mentions the Law no less than five times (Lk 2:22, 23, 24, 27, 39). Luke wants to be certain you know that Jesus perfectly fulfilled the Law God gave to Moses.

Two other things happened that day. As Mary and Joseph were presenting Jesus to the Lord so that He may be called "holy—the Son of God" (Lk 1:35) as Gabriel announced, a man named Simeon entered the temple. He was filled with the Holy Spirit. The Holy Spirit revealed to Simeon that he would not die until he saw the Promised Child, the Lord's Christ. Not only did Simeon see the Promised Child, but he actually held Him! Simeon takes baby Jesus in his arms and says something like "Lord, I can now die in peace and joy because I have held Your Promised Child in the palms of my hands." His actual words, known as "The Nunc Dimittis," are far more eloquent and profound. He says,

> **Lord, now You are letting Your servant depart in peace, according to Your word; for my eyes have seen Your salvation that You have prepared in the presence of all peoples, a light for revelation to the Gentiles, and for glory to Your people Israel. (Lk 2:29–32)**

After saying this, Simeon reveals to Mary that many people in Israel would believe that Jesus is the Promised Child. But many would also reject Him. And that rejection would be a sword that would pierce Mary's soul.

Additionally, there was also an eighty-four-year-old widow from the tribe of Asher in the temple that day. Her name was Anna. She was in the temple fasting and praying. Upon hearing the words of Simeon, Anna thanks God for this gift of the Promised Child who has finally come. Then she ecstatically tells "all who were waiting for the redemption of Jerusalem" (Lk 2:38) about the infant Jesus.

The third story of Jesus' childhood occurs sometime before He was two years old (see Mt 2:16). Sometime after Jesus' birth, Gentile foreigners, Magi, travel to Jerusalem in search of a king. They're not searching for just any king, but rather the one "who has been born king of the Jews"

(Mt 2:2). They search for the Christ the prophet Micah foresaw, the Christ born in the humble town of Bethlehem, the Christ who would rule over God's people, Israel, as shepherd (see Mi 5:2–4), the One whose birth caused a star to appear in the sky. After a brief encounter with King Herod of Jerusalem, the Magi head off toward Bethlehem to continue their search. Guided by the star this time, the Magi enter the house to see the child with Mary. And at this, all the Magi fall down and worship the child. How many fall down? Scripture never tells us the number of Magi. What we do know is that these Magi bring three kingly gifts: gold, frankincense, and myrrh (see Mt 2:11).

The Magi are then warned in a dream not to return to Herod to tell him where to find this newborn king as he instructed. Their absence provokes Herod's anger. So much so that he orders the death of all male children in Bethlehem who are two years old and younger. What happens to the Promised Child, Christ the King? While the Bethlehem mothers wept at the death of their children as Jeremiah foresaw, Jesus, God's Son, escaped to Egypt as Hosea foresaw (see Jer 31:15; Hos 11:1). Mary, Joseph, and Jesus lived there until Herod's death. Then they moved to Nazareth.

Jesus' final childhood narrative occurs when He is twelve years old. While traveling home from their annual Passover pilgrimage to Jerusalem, Mary and Joseph notice that Jesus is not among their relatives. He is missing. After they return to Jerusalem and search for three days, Mary and Joseph

Figure 6: The King

find Jesus exactly where they left Him, in the temple. The crowd is all amazed by the understanding and answers Jesus gives to questions asked in the temple. But Mary and Joseph are perplexed by what Jesus says to them: "Did you not know that I must be in My Father's house?" (Lk 2:49). They don't understand that Jesus is calling God His Father and the temple God's house. Irrespective, Jesus returns to Nazareth with them. Luke also notes that He is submissive to them and grows in wisdom, stature, and favor "with God and man" (Lk 2:52).

Subsequently, we know that Jesus' childhood was like ours, ordinarily human. He ate. He slept. He traveled. He enjoyed time with His parents. He celebrated religious festivals. Yet unlike us, Jesus is perfect like His Heavenly Father and holy like the temple. For He actively obeys and fulfills God's Law perfectly (see Mt 5:17). Furthermore, He is God's Son, Christ the King, who has come and would later ride into Jerusalem on a donkey to save His people from their sins as foretold by the Old Testament prophets.

For the next eighteen years of Jesus' life, Scripture is silent. It is silent until Jesus begins His ministry by being baptized by John in the Jordan River. I know, being baptized by John seems odd since John's Baptism is for the forgiveness of sins and Jesus is perfect. It seemed odd to John too. For John recognized that Jesus didn't need to have sins taken away. He is the one who takes away sin. Jesus is "the Lamb of God, who takes away the sin of the world" (Jn 1:29). That is why when Jesus came to him, John said, "I need to be baptized by You, and do You come to me?" (Mt 3:14). Jesus' answer is profound. He said, "Let it be so now, for thus it is fitting for us to fulfill all righteousness" (Mt 3:15). In essence, "Yes, John, I know. But this is what it means to be the Lamb of God. So come now. Let us go down to the water. Confess Israel's sins over Me and pour them on Me so that I can take them away. So that I can sanctify them. For this is how I make them holy."

And with that, Jesus and John enter the water. Upon Jesus' Baptism, the heavens are torn open (see Mk 1:10). The Holy Spirit descends on Him in the bodily form of a dove (see Lk 3:22). And the Father's voice resounds, "This is My beloved Son, with whom I am well pleased" (1Jn 4:14). Here, at the Baptism of our Lord, we see the one true God—Father, Son, and Holy Spirit—at work for the salvation of the world. The Father has sent the Son in the power of the Holy Spirit to be the Savior of the world.

Having passed through the waters of Baptism, with Israel's sin now squarely on His shoulders, Jesus is sent out by God into the wilderness. After fasting forty days and forty nights, He is tempted by the devil. Just as God's created sons Adam (see Lk 3:38) and the nation of Israel (see Ex 4:22) were tempted with food, so Jesus, God's only-begotten Son, the first-born of Mary, was tempted with food. But where Adam selfishly succumbed and Israel self-centeredly grumbled, Jesus selflessly waits. As hungry as He is, He will not turn the stones into bread. He will trust the Father. He will live "by every word that comes from the mouth of God" (Mt 4:4).

The second temptation takes place on the pinnacle of the temple. Satan invites Jesus to jump, and then quickly reassures Him, with words from Psalm 91, that the angels will protect Him. But Jesus knows that Satan is "the father of lies" (Jn 8:44) and does not quote God's Word correctly. Jesus knows that Psalm 91 is God's promise of protection from enemies, not self-imposed reckless living. He will not test God, like Israel did at Massah and Meribah. Hence, He quotes Deuteronomy 6:16: "You shall not put the Lord your God to the test" (Mt 4:7).

The final temptation occurs on a tall mountain where Satan shows Him "all the kingdoms of the world and their glory" (Mt 4:8). Satan promises Jesus that these can belong to Him if Jesus simply worships him. In one respect, this seems like a ludicrous and idiotic request since the world and everything in it belongs to

Figure 7: The True Israel

God (see Ps 24:1), and Jesus is God. But in another respect, it is extremely pointed. After all, the sin that Israel has succumbed to all along is idolatry. They constantly break the First Commandment, failing to "fear, love, and trust in God above all things."[26] Moreover, "whoever makes a practice of sinning is of the devil" (1Jn 3:8), "the whole world lies in the power of the evil one" (1Jn 5:19), and Jesus was sent to save the world. The temptation then is to save the world, not by crushing the serpent's head as the Father sent Him to do, but by giving into the serpent and worshiping him. Unlike Israel, which whored after any and all gods, Jesus, the only-begotten Son, the true Israel, remains faithful to His Father's Word. He worships and serves God alone. Like Adam, Israel, and us, Jesus is tempted. Yet unlike us all, Jesus is without sin (see Heb 4:15).

Not only was Jesus sinless, but He spoke and taught as "one who had authority, and not as the scribes" (Mk 1:22). While walking by the Sea of Galilee, Jesus called to Andrew and Simon, also known as Peter. "Follow Me," He said, "and I will make you fishers of men" (Mt 4:19). And they followed Him immediately. The same can be said of James, John, Philip, Bartholomew, Thomas, Matthew, James the son of Alphaeus, Thaddaeus, Simon the Zealot, and Judas Iscariot. Jesus called, and at His Word, they left everything and followed Him.

As Jesus preached a sermon to the mountainside crowd, touching on several commandments from God's Law, they were absolutely astonished. He taught them in a way they had never experienced. Instead of citing people and passages to establish authority, like the scribes and Pharisees, Jesus spoke with His authority: "You have heard that it was said. . . . But I say to you . . . " (Mt 5:21–22, 27–28). And, "It was also said. . . . But I say to you" (Mt 5:31–32). He spoke to them as if He authored the Law.

Even those who sought to trap Him were confounded. For when a pharisaical lawyer asked Jesus, "Which is the great commandment in the Law?" (Mt 22:36), he expected Jesus to pick one. The Pharisee could then make a fool of Him for putting one law above another. However, Jesus responds by simply telling the lawyer to love God and love your neighbor, because "on these two commandments depend all the Law and the Prophets" (Mt 22:40). In essence, "all God's commandments are important. And they are easily summarized. Love God. This is the First Table of the Law:

26 Small Catechism, First Commandment

commandments one through three. It affects your relationship with God. It is the greatest. Also, love your neighbor. This is the Second Table of the Law: commandments four through ten. This affects your relationship with your neighbor. It, too, is the greatest. This is what I teach. This is what I gave Moses and the Prophets. So quit playing games. Stop pitting God's Law against itself and against Me. Obey it perfectly."

The divine authority with which Jesus spoke and taught undoubtedly caused all who heard it to marvel. But the miracles He performed with that same authority caused people to wonder in awe, "Who is this man?" While over thirty miracles of Jesus can be counted in the four Gospels—Matthew, Mark, Luke, and John—only five are necessary to sufficiently answer that question.

The first miracle happens one evening while Jesus is out on a boat with His disciples. Suddenly, a great windstorm ensues, and waves begin crashing into the boat. The disciples are terrified. They don't want to be capsized. They don't want to drown in the storm. But Jesus? He's not concerned at all. He is sleeping on a cushion in the stern of the boat. Terrified of certain death, the disciples wake Him. "Teacher," they say, "do You not care that we are perishing?" (Mk 4:38). Of course He does. Which is why He awakens and speaks. "Peace! Be Still!" (Mk 4:39). At His word, just like in the Garden of Eden, creation obeys. The wind ceases. The water stills. All is calm. And the disciples tremulously murmur, "Who then is this, that even the wind and the sea obey Him?" (Mk 4:41).

The second miracle takes place after Jesus finishes preaching the Sermon on the Mount. As He is coming down the mountain, an unclean leper (see Lv 13:44–45) approaches Jesus, kneels before Him, and asks to be made clean. Jesus does for this leper what no one else would. He has compassion on him. He speaks, "I will; be clean" (Mt 8:3). And then He mercifully touches the leper. But it is not Jesus who becomes unclean or even ill. It is the leper who is made clean. For at Jesus' word, and by His touch, the illness is undone.

The third miracle occurs while Jesus is teaching. People from all over Galilee, Judea, and Jerusalem have come to hear Him, as have the Pharisees. The crowd was so large that the men who were carrying a paralytic to Jesus for healing couldn't even get close to Him. So they climb up on the roof of the building. Then they lower the paralytic through the tiles, bed and all, until he lay before Jesus. Responding to the faith of these men, Jesus says, "Man, your sins are forgiven you" (Lk 5:20). The Pharisees and scribes are outraged by Jesus' response. "Who is this who speaks blasphemies? Who can forgive sins but God alone?" (Lk 5:21), they all think to them-selves. But Jesus knows their thoughts. While it would have been easier to tell the paralyzed man to "rise and walk," Jesus chooses the more difficult phrase so that they "may know that the Son of Man has authority on earth to forgive sins" (Lk 5:23). But before they can even respond, Jesus speaks to the paralyzed man, "I say to you, rise, pick up your bed and go home" (Lk 5:24). And by His word, both the ability and strength to walk skillfully and effortlessly are imparted. The formerly paralyzed man quickly stands, carries his bed, and glorifies God as he strides home.

The fourth miracle transpires at a synagogue in Capernaum. As Jesus begins teaching, a demon-possessed man who had been sitting and listening fearfully cries, "What have You to do with us, Jesus of Nazareth? Have You come to destroy us? I know who You are—the Holy One of God" (Mk 1:24). Jesus, however, simply rebukes the demon, commanding it to be quiet and come out. The demon submissively obeys Jesus' authorita-tive word and is cast out.

The final miracle happens in the small village of Bethany, located two miles east of Jerusalem. Jesus' friend Lazarus had previously been ill but was now four days dead and in the tomb. When Jesus and the disciples arrive, Lazarus's sister Martha greets Him with lament: "Lord, if You had been here, my brother would not have died" (Jn 11:21). But Jesus greets her with great joy. "Your brother will rise again" (Jn 11:23), He says. She knows that Lazarus will rise on the Last Day. But what Martha doesn't know is that the resurrection isn't about a day—it is about a person. Jesus, who stands before her, is "the resurrection and the life" (Jn 11:25). Yet even Jesus sorrows as He beholds the great enemy, death, which humanity brought into this world through our fall into sin. He weeps because this is not the way things are supposed to be. We weren't created to die. We were created to live with God forever. And to that end, to the glory of God, Jesus commands that the stone in front of Lazarus's tomb be taken away. He then tells Lazarus to "come out" (Jn 11:43). At this, the four-day-dead and decomposing man hears Jesus' words, and death is undone. Lazarus walks out of the tomb and lives.

Who is this man? He is the one who has power over creation, illness, sin, Satan, and even death. He speaks, and they must submit to and obey His authoritative word. He does things only God can do. Consequently, this Jesus is none other than God in the flesh.

And what Jesus does for one man, Lazarus, He desires to do for the whole world. God "desires all people to be saved and to come to the knowledge of the truth" (1Tm 2:4). He desires that "everyone who looks on the Son and believes in Him should have eternal life" and be raised from the dead on the Last Day (see Jn 6:39–40). In order for that to happen, Jesus must first free us from our slavery. Not slavery to the Egyptians, Assyrians, or Babylonians, but to a far older and much greater enemy, sin (see Jn 8:34; Rm 6:16–20).

This is why throughout His entire ministry, Jesus told His disciples that "the Son of Man must suffer many things and be rejected by the elders and chief priests and scribes, and be killed, and on the third day be raised" (Lk 9:22). This is what Jesus was discussing with Moses and Elijah on the Mount of Transfiguration when His appearance was changed and He radiantly shone with the light of God's glory. Jesus spoke to all of them about His exodus (see Lk 9:31).

I know that sounds strange because when you hear the word *exodus*, you think of a particular individual piece of this puzzle. You think of Moses, slavery, Egypt, the death of the firstborn, and God's passing over Israel, sparing them from His judgment of death and giving the gift of life on account of the blood of the lamb. But it is not strange. For, as you know, God works in remarkably consistent and reminiscent ways. He takes key elements of His work from the major historical Old Testament events in God's story of salvation and uses them to bring about something new and more substantive. So that what God did for a few people in the Old Testament, He now does for all people in the person and work of Jesus. Thus, when the life and work of Jesus are held up to these Old Testament events, they are illuminated. And suddenly you begin to see that these stories are not independent. The Old Testament stories are the shadows, but the substance or reality is Christ (see Col 2:17; Rm 5:14). In Christ, everything and everyone is intricately connected and held together (see Col 1:17). In Christ, all things work together to proclaim God's breathtakingly beautiful story of salvation for us that began all the way back in Genesis.

Figure 8: The Lamb

How do the key elements of the exodus narrative and Jesus' crucifixion connect? Well, as God issued a judgment of death upon all sinners in Egypt, so that same edict stands for all people throughout all time. "The wages of sin is death" (Rm 6:23). And as God mercifully and lovingly spares those who believe in Him, His chosen people, from His judgment through the sacrifice of an appropriately sized unblemished male lamb's blood (see Ex 12:5), so also God continues to spare all believers, His chosen people (see 1Pt 2:5–10; Jn 3:17), from His judgment through Jesus, the perfect and sinless male Lamb of God, whose blood was smeared on the vertical and horizontal wooden beams—the post and lintel—of the cross. Moreover, as the Passover lamb did not have its bones broken, neither does Jesus have His legs broken. He is pierced in the side with a spear to ascertain death (see Jn 19:32–37). By His death and through His blood, we have not only been spared from the judgment, or wrath, of God (see Rm 5:9; 6:23) but we have been set free (see Jn 8:35–36). We are no longer "enslaved to sin" (Rm 6:6).

The key element of Jesus as the sacrificial Lamb of God also connects to and illumines another piece of the Old Testament narrative, namely the tabernacle and temple. While we know the flesh of Jesus is the new temple, or dwelling place of God, we do not yet know His work in the temple. As the sins of the people were placed on the scapegoat, so also the sins of the world, throughout all time, were placed upon Jesus at His Baptism. And as the annual scapegoat and the bodies of the animals from Israel's daily sin offerings were taken outside the Israelite camp and away from the temple, so also was Jesus taken outside Israel's capital city of Jerusalem, away from the Jerusalem temple, to suffer and die outside the camp (see Heb 13:12–13) on the hill of Golgotha (see Mt 27:33). There, in the temple of His body, Jesus, our merciful and faithful high priest (see Heb 2:17), entered into the eternal holy place, once for all, to offer Himself (see Heb 9:12–28) as the lamb of sacrifice to atone for the sins of the world (see 1Jn 2:2) while praying, "Father, forgive them" (Lk 23:34). After the work of His sacrifice was completed, after "it is finished" (Jn 19:28–30), we who were once far off and separated from God were brought near and reconciled to Him by the blood of Jesus (see Eph 2:13; 2Co 5:19). Our hearts have been sprinkled clean. Our sins have been removed from us and scattered "as far as the east is from the west" (Ps 103:12). We are justified by His blood (see Rm 5:9). We are pure and holy, without spot, wrinkle, or blemish (see Eph 5:27). And the curtain of the temple has been torn in two from top to bottom (see Mk 15:38). The dividing wall of hostility has been broken down (see Eph 2:14). We now have access to the Father (see Eph 2:18).

This is precisely what the Father sent His only-begotten Son to do. For God loved the world in this way, "that He gave His only Son" (Jn 3:16). "He . . . did not spare His own Son but gave Him up for us all" (Rm 8:32). And Jesus, anointed with the Spirit, sought to do the Father's will (see Jn 5:30). He even prayed for its fulfillment in the Garden of Gethsemane on the night Judas betrayed Him (see Mk 14:36). What's more, He submitted Himself to it. Having taken the form of our suffering servant, Jesus "was despised and rejected by men" (Is 53:3). He was abandoned by His own disciples (see Mt 26:56). Peter denied even knowing Him (see Lk 22:54–61). His own people—the chief priests, scribes, Pharisees, and the crowds— falsely accused Him and cried out for His death. Pilate washed his hands of Him, had Him scourged with whips, and delivered Him over to be crucified (see Mt 27:24–26). The soldiers mocked Him, crowned Him with thorns, and casts lots to gain possession of His clothing (see Jn 19:2–3, 23–24). Yet He willingly bore their sins, as He bore yours and mine. Jesus bore the sins of the world. Thus, as Abraham's son Isaac carried the wood of sacrifice on his back and was laid out on it, so Jesus carried His own cross and was laid on it (see Jn 19:17). "And as Moses lifted up the serpent in the wilderness, so must the Son of Man be lifted up" (Jn 3:14). Jesus was obedient to the will of His Father even unto death on the cross (see Php 2:8). Now everyone who looks to Jesus, everyone who believes in Him will "not perish but have eternal life" (Jn 3:15–16). He is the source of our eternal salvation (see Heb 5:9). Jesus is our Savior.

Figure 9: The Savior

After Jesus breathed His last breath and gave up the Holy Spirit, Joseph of Arimathea, with Pilate's permission, took Jesus' body to prepare it for burial (see Jn 19:30, 38). He and a Pharisee named Nicodemus wrapped Jesus' body in linen strips with about seventy-five pounds of spices (see Jn 19:39–40). As God rested after He had finished the work of creation, so Jesus, having finished the work of our salvation, rests. He is laid in an unused tomb near where He was crucified (see Jn 19:41–42). A great stone was rolled in front of the tomb's entrance and at the request of the chief priests and Pharisees, soldiers were posted at the tomb to secure it "until the third day" (Mt 27:60–66). And as Jonah spent three days and nights in the belly of the great fish, so Jesus would spend three days and three nights in the heart of the earth, just as He said (see Mt 12:38–40).

But on the third day, the dawning of the first day of a new week, when Mary Magdalene and Mary, the mother of James and Joseph, arrive at the tomb with spices in hand expecting to find death, they find life. For the angel who had rolled back the great stone says to them, "Do not be afraid, for I know that you seek Jesus who was crucified. He is not here, for He has risen, as He said. Come, see the place where He lay" (Mt 28:5–6). And once they peer into the tomb, they see that Jesus' body is not there (see Lk 24:3). When they run and tell the disciples what they have seen, as the angel commanded them, Peter and John hasten to the tomb (see Mt 28:8; Jn 20:1–4). But they do not find Jesus' body either. They find empty linen cloths, as well as Jesus' face cloth folded neatly and placed to the side (see Jn 20:5–7). And when Jesus calls Mary Magdalene by name while she is weeping outside of His tomb, her tremendous sorrow is transformed into inestimable joy.

Jesus lives! The grave could not hold Him (see Ac 2:24). Death has no dominion over Him (see Rm 6:9). Christ has trampled down death—by death.[27] He used the serpent's own weapon against him. Thus, the serpent who overcame by the tree of the garden was likewise overcome by the tree of the cross.[28] The serpent's head is crushed. Jesus, who defeated the devil, has the power over death and has delivered us from our slavery (see Heb 2:14–15). Just as Israel's enemy, Pharaoh and his army, were swallowed by the Red Sea, so our much older, stronger, and greater enemy, death, is swallowed up in the victory of the resurrection (see 1Co 15:54). By Jesus' glorious resurrection He has "abolished death and brought life and immortality to light" (2Tm 1:10).

During the forty days after His resurrection, Jesus appeared to many people and proclaimed His victory over sin, death, and the devil. He appeared to Cleopas and another disciple who were discussing Jesus' crucifixion as they were walking to Emmaus. He explained that it was necessary for the Christ to suffer and then enter His glory (see Lk 24:25–26). Later that evening, He appeared to His disciples, who were cowering behind a locked door in fear of the Jews. Though Thomas was absent at the time, Jesus appeared among them and said, "Peace be with you" (Jn 20:19). As they gazed at the wounds on Jesus' hands and side, they erupted in joy. For they had seen the crucified and now risen Christ. Eight days later, He appeared to them all again. This time however, Thomas was present and

---

27 Orthodox Church in America, "Common Prayers—Selected Liturgical Hymns," The Paschal Troparion, https://www.oca.org/orthodoxy/prayers/selected-liturgical-hymns (accessed January 18, 2022).

28 *LSB Altar Book*, p. 231.

got to touch the wounds on Jesus' hands and side. When He did, his rank unbelief was transformed to fragrant faith (see Jn 20:28). Later, as Peter, Thomas, Nathanael, James, and John were fishing in the Sea of Tiberias, Jesus called to them from the shore. He allowed them to catch 153 fish. He prepared a breakfast of fish and bread for them. He ate with them. And then He mercifully and lovingly forgave Peter for denying Him when He asked him not once, not twice, but three times, "Do you love Me?" (Jn 21:15–19). Jesus even appeared to over five hundred people at one time (see 1Co 15:6).

When the forty days were over, Jesus led His disciples out of Jerusalem. They went as far as Bethany (see Lk 24:50). Then suddenly, as Jesus was speaking to them and blessing them, He was "carried up into heaven" (Lk 24:51). Jesus ascended to the right hand of the Father (see Ac 2:33; 7:55;

1Pt 3:22) in the flesh (see Lk 24:39). The Father exalted Him and bestowed upon Him the name that is above every name (see Php 2:9; Eph 1:21).

The disciples, however, didn't understand this at first, even though Jesus had told them on the night He was betrayed that He was "going to the Father" (Jn 14:28). They had to be asked by two men why they were just standing there looking into heaven. They had to be told that Jesus would return from heaven in the same way He was taken up (see Ac 1:11). Jesus had even promised them that when He returned, He would take them, and all believers, to be with Him so that where He is, we will be also (see Jn 14:3).

On the Last Day, Jesus "will descend from heaven with a cry of command, with the voice of an archangel, and with the sound of the trumpet of God" (1Th 4:16). When the trumpet sounds, the dead will be raised (see Jn 5:28–29). Our mortal and perishable bodies will be raised immortal and imperishable (see 1Co 15:52–54). Then all believers in Jesus will hear Him say, "Come, you who are blessed by My Father, inherit the kingdom prepared for you from the foundation of the world" (Mt 25:34). And we will. We will enter eternal life to physically and intimately dwell with God (see Rv 21:3–4). There will be no more mourning, crying, pain, or death. There will simply be eternal life with the eternal Lord. What Adam lost, Christ will have forever restored.

This is why the Father had sent the Son in the power of the Holy Spirit. This is why the Son took on flesh in the Virgin's womb and was named Jesus. This is why Jesus suffered, bled, died, rose, and ascended to the Father's right hand. All of this happened so that God's fallen creation may "live under Him in His Kingdom."[29] This is God's great story of salvation from Genesis to Revelation. Truly, God has joined us in the flesh so that we may join Him in our flesh in eternity.

---

29 Small Catechism, Second Article

CHAPTER 6

ONE IN CHRIST

As wonderful as God's great story of salvation from Genesis to Revelation is, one crucial problem remains. While Jesus has promised to return to take us to be with Him, the reality is that He has not yet returned. God's story has not yet ended. Thus, we find ourselves neither in the beautiful beginning nor the triumphal end of the story. Rather, we find ourselves precisely in the murky middle. Murky because now that Jesus has ascended to the Father's right hand, we can no longer see Him face-to-face. Postascension and preresurrection of all flesh, He is veiled from our eyes. So we, like the people of God in the Old Testament, must ask once again, "Where is the Promised Child who has crushed the head of the serpent, and when will He return to restore to us the unveiled presence of God?" We, like the disciples, are left wondering, "Where are You, God?"

Yet despite the inherent sorrow and desolation that Israel, the disciples, and even we may feel as we wait, watch, and wonder about God's presence among us, the truth is that God has not abandoned us. Though Jesus is veiled from our sight, He has not left us as orphans. He has still given us a way to encounter Him, means by which we may touch, hear, taste, smell, and see Him. Put differently, even though Jesus has ascended to the right hand of God to intercede for us as our great High Priest (see Rm 8:34), He still comes down to dwell with us here in time even as we await His return.

"How?" you might wonder. Well, in the most remarkable way. God uses the foolish things in the world to shame the wise and the weak things of this world to shame the strong (see 1Co 1:27). He took a virgin and made her His mother. He took a feeding trough and made it His bed. He took a donkey and made it His noble steed by which He entered Jerusalem. He took a tree of death—a cross—and made it a tree of life. He took a barren and desolate place of mortality—a tomb—and made it a fertile and fruitful place of immortality. Now, upon His ascension, He takes cowardly fishermen and makes them bold and enlivened fishers of men.

For this transformation to occur, both on the night in which He was betrayed and right before His ascension, Jesus promised His disciples that they would receive the Holy Spirit (see Jn 14:26; 16:7; Ac 1:5). The Spirit would continually guide the disciples "into all truth" (Jn 16:13). That is, the Spirit would allow them to accurately and completely remember, understand, and believe all that they had heard, seen, and received from

Jesus, who is "the way, and the truth, and the life" (Jn 14:6). The Spirit would enable them to boldly confess that "Jesus is Lord" (1Co 12:3), not only in their own lives but before the world and for all to hear. Once they had received the Holy Spirit and were fully "clothed with power from on high" (Lk 24:49), the disciples would be Jesus' witnesses "in Jerusalem and in all Judea and Samaria, and to the end of the earth" (Ac 1:8). Through these men, repentance and the forgiveness of sins in Jesus' name would be proclaimed to all nations, just as He promised (see Lk 24:47).

This is why Jesus appeared to the disciples, who were cowering behind locked doors in fear of the Jews that Easter evening. He stood among them, proclaimed peace to them, and showed them His hands and side to prove His bodily resurrection. Then Jesus called them to serve in His stead and by His command. Knowing that He would soon ascend to the Father, Jesus said, "As the Father has sent Me, even so I am sending you" (Jn 20:21). Then, just as God breathed into Adam's nostrils that he might live (see Gn 2:7), so Jesus breathes upon the disciples so that all people may not die but have eternal life (see Jn 20:22; 3:16). "Receive the Holy Spirit," Jesus says. "If you forgive the sins of any, they are forgiven them; if you withhold forgiveness from any, it is withheld" (Jn 20:22–23). With these words and with His Spirit, Jesus commends His ministry of reconciliation to these disciples (see 2Co 5:19–20). He calls them into His Office of the Holy Ministry.

As the Father sent the Son in the power of the Holy Spirit to accomplish the work of salvation through His sacrificial death on the cross, by which comes the forgiveness of all sins, so now Jesus sends these men in the power of the Holy Spirit to give out or withhold that forgiveness. These disciples are called by Jesus to continue His ministry. They are His instruments. Through them, Christ continues to speak and absolve, or forgive, sins. Hence, whoever hears them hears Jesus, and whoever rejects them rejects Jesus and the Father who sent Him (see Lk 10:16).

Out on the Galilean mountain, Jesus speaks to the disciples again. "Go therefore and make disciples of all nations," He says, "baptizing them in the name of the Father and of the Son and of the Holy Spirit, teaching them to observe all that I have commanded you" (Mt 28:19–20). Specifically, Jesus sends these eleven disciples into all the world. They are given the responsibility of baptizing and continually teaching everyone who hears them, both Jew and Gentile, about God's message of salvation for all people in Jesus Christ. As they do these things, Jesus assures them that since all authority on heaven and earth has been given to Him, they will make disciples, or believers. He even concretely ties His presence to them and to all who receive His Baptism and teaching from them. "Behold, I am with you always, to the end of the age," Jesus says (Mt 28:20). Subsequently, it is Jesus who is present with and makes disciples from every nation, from all tribes, peoples, and languages, as He baptizes and teaches through these apostolic eyewitnesses.

In addition to pronouncing absolution, baptizing, teaching, and preaching Jesus Christ crucified and risen for the forgiveness of sins and the life of the world, these disciples are given one final responsibility. On the night in which Jesus was betrayed, He took the unleavened bread of the Passover meal. After blessing it, Jesus broke it and gave it to the disciples and said, "Take, eat; this is My body" (Mt 26:26). Then, He took the cup of wine and gave it to them and said, "Drink of it, all of you, for this is My blood of the covenant, which is poured out for many for the forgiveness of sins" (Mt 26:27–28). The giving and receiving of this bread-body of Jesus and the wine-blood of Jesus was not meant to be a onetime event. It was instituted to be a continual, ongoing celebration of His presence. That is why in the middle of this most holy supper, Jesus commanded His disciples, "Do this in remembrance of Me" (Lk 22:19).

Through the regular administration and reception of the Lord's Supper, Jesus invites these disciples, and all who join them, to touch, taste, smell, hear, and see Golgotha. He invites them to eat and drink His very body and blood, which was given and shed for the forgiveness of sins. As often as they eat and drink this meal, they participate in Jesus' sacrifice (see 1Co 10:16), proclaim His death (see 1Co 11:26), receive the fruit of forgiveness from His cross, and dwell with Him at His table (see 1Co 10:21; 11:24–25).

That God would use the foolish and weak things of this world—sinful disciples who themselves need to be forgiven, words, water, bread, and wine—to continue to dwell with us and give us His gifts of forgiveness and life after His ascension is of tremendous importance and great comfort. For if Jesus uses these sinful men as His chosen instruments to proclaim His death and resurrection, then we can be assured that Jesus still comes to save sinners (see 1Tm 1:15)! If He equips these fishers of men with common, everyday tools such as words, water, bread, and wine, then we can be confident that salvation is in fact for all people, and its power and certainty rest solely on Jesus (see 1Co 1:28–29). And if these tools are tangible and can be experienced with our senses, then we can be certain that Jesus remains present with us in these Means of Grace—His Word, Holy Absolution, Holy Baptism, and Holy Communion—until the end of the age. He is as near to us as the sound in our ears, the sight and feeling of water poured on our heads, and the taste and smell of bread and wine in our mouths.

These seemingly weak and foolish things are then neither weak nor foolish. They deliver the Gospel to us: Jesus Christ crucified and risen for the forgiveness of sins and the life of the world. They are the very power of God for the salvation of all who believe in Him (see Rm 1:16). Postascension and preresurrection of all flesh, this is how Jesus promised that He would be with us and continue to draw all people to Himself, that He might have a people for His own possession, a holy nation, a royal priesthood (see 1Pt 2:9).

While the Office of the Holy Ministry and the administration of the Means of Grace were instituted by Jesus before His ascension, their enactment through the disciples did not begin until ten days later. Jews from every nation were gathered in Jerusalem to celebrate the harvest festival of the Feast of Weeks (see Nu 28:26–31) as Moses had commanded. The disciples had returned to Jerusalem and were waiting as Jesus had instructed them. They had even called another apostolic eyewitness named Matthias to share in Jesus' ministry since Judas had hung himself (see Ac 1:15–26). On Pentecost, the fiftieth day after Jesus' resurrection, while the Jews were still celebrating the harvest festival, the sound of a mighty wind filled the house where the disciples were gathered. Tongues of fire rested on each of the twelve apostles. They were suddenly clothed with the power from on high or "filled with the Holy Spirit," and each disciple began to speak in the specific languages of nations who were gathered in Jerusalem (see Ac 2:3–4).

What did the Twelve say? Well, they proclaimed or bore witness to the mighty works of God in Jesus Christ. But those who heard them weren't initially focused on what they said. They were focused on the fact that these twelve Galilean men, who had not studied a foreign language, were suddenly speaking all these foreign languages fluently. Amazed and perplexed by this, the crowd asked one another, "What does this mean?" (Ac 2:12).

Two explanations are given. The first explanation is that these men were drunk. It sounds foolish, doesn't it? Foolish because anyone who has ever heard drunkards speak knows that they don't suddenly speak an unlearned foreign language fluently and intelligibly. They slur gibberish. Sadly, this was the intent of those who offered the first explanation. They rejected Jesus. And then they mocked His disciples.

The second explanation is given by one of the Twelve. When Peter heard the ridicule, he reacted. He declared that the men were not drunk since it was only nine o'clock in the morning. He asserted that the very thing they mocked was actually foretold by the prophet Joel and was being fulfilled. God was pouring out His Spirit on all flesh so "that everyone who calls upon the name of the Lord shall be saved" (Ac 2:21). Having explained the sudden wind, fire, and ability to speak foreign languages fluently, which captivated the crowd, Peter focused their attention on the heart of the matter—the mighty works of God that the disciples were declaring.

He proclaimed that "Jesus of Nazareth, a man attested to you by God with mighty works and wonders and signs that God did through Him in your midst . . . you crucified and killed by the hands of lawless men" (Ac 2:22–23). However, Peter also announced that since it was impossible for death to hold Him, God raised Him up and "made Him both Lord and Christ, this Jesus whom you crucified" (Ac 2:36). When the crowd heard the first part of Peter's sermon, they were terrified of God's judgment upon their sin and cried out in repentance, "What shall we do?" (Ac 2:37).

Peter, however, did not leave the crowd in their sin. For Jesus didn't send the Twelve to preach repentance only. He sent them to preach repentance for the forgiveness of sins in His name, beginning with Jerusalem. He sent them to proclaim the forgiveness of sins to repentant sinners. So to those who were cut to the heart, Peter continued to preach Jesus Christ and Him crucified and risen for the forgiveness of all their sins. "Repent and be baptized every one of you in the name of Jesus Christ for the forgiveness of your sins, and you will receive the gift of the Holy

Spirit," he says (Ac 2:38). And since faith comes by hearing the word of Christ (see Rm 10:17), about three thousand people who heard Peter's sermon believed. They underwent Baptism, received the Holy Spirit, and were saved. Through preaching and Baptism, Jesus made disciples from the nations. He continued to assemble His Church, a people He obtained with His own blood (see Ac 20:28).

This may be the first instance of Jesus gaining a people for His own possession in Jerusalem, but it is not the last. One afternoon at about three o'clock, when Peter and John were going to the temple to pray, they encountered a paralyzed man asking for alms at the temple gate. They did not have any silver or gold to give him. However, they did give him the one thing that they had, Jesus. "In the name of Jesus Christ of Nazareth, rise up and walk," Peter proclaimed (Ac 3:6). Immediately, the paralyzed man leaped up and accompanied Peter and John into the temple. All who saw this were amazed and wondered what had happened. But before the crowd could concoct a story about the healing or ascribe it to these two disciples, Peter interjected. He preached Jesus. He said that it is not by their own power or piety that the lame man walked but by Jesus, the God of Abraham, Isaac, and Jacob, whom they crucified. He called them to repent of this, turn back to God, and have their sins blotted out. And about five thousand men who heard the preached Word believed (see Ac 4:4).

However, not everyone who heard the word of the Lord that day came to faith. The temple priests, captain, and Sadducees who overheard Peter preach Jesus Christ crucified and risen for the forgiveness of sins were "greatly annoyed" (Ac 4:1–2). They proceeded to question Peter and John about it. And while they were astonished at the boldness of Peter and John, still they didn't want to hear about Jesus. They forbade the disciples from speaking or teaching in His name and threatened to punish them if they did it again.

Irrespective, the disciples are not deterred. They are Jesus' chosen instruments. They are His witnesses. They "must obey God rather than men" (Ac 5:29). They must preach the Gospel since "there is salvation in no one else, for there is no other name [besides Jesus] under heaven given among men by which we must be saved" (Ac 4:12). Moreover, Jesus had not given them the Spirit of timidity but of power, love, and self-control (see 2Tm 1:7). Consequently, the Twelve "did not cease teaching and preaching that the Christ is Jesus" (Ac 5:42), even if that meant imprison-ment, floggings, and death. And as they continued to preach and teach the Word of Christ, the Holy Spirit repeatedly increased the number of those who were being saved day by day.

During this time, the Church in Jerusalem grew so large that it was impossible for the Twelve to preach, teach, and care for everyone. There was even a complaint from the believing Hellenistic Jews that the Christian widows were neglected in the daily food distribution. To rectify this, the Lord called more men to assist in the Office of the Holy Ministry. Only this time, Jesus, "the Lord of the harvest" (Mt 9:38), didn't call them into His Office immediately by appearing, speaking to them, and bestowing the Holy Spirit upon them face-to-face. This time, He chose to call them medi-ately, that is by means of His Church, both pastor and people. Therefore, the Twelve called the entire assembly of believers in Jerusalem together and instructed them to choose seven men from the gathered assembly (see Ac 6:3).

However, they could not simply pick anyone they wanted but only those who met specific qualifications. Like the twelve apostles, they had to be men who were dignified, sober-minded, publicly blameless, and the husband of one wife. They were not to select anyone who was a drunkard, double-tongued, greedy, slanderous, or one whose household was in disarray and whose children were disobedient (see 1Tm 3:8–13). Succinctly put, they needed to publicly be known as men "of good repute, full of the Spirit and of wisdom" (Ac 6:3) since they were Jesus' represen-tatives, standing in His stead and by His command.

Accordingly, the people selected Stephen, Philip, Prochorus, Nicanor, Timon, Parmenas, and Nicolaus and placed them before the apostles. The Twelve then ordained, or publicly recognized, appointed, and conferred the Office upon these men by publicly praying for and laying their hands on them.[30] These seven men were to serve in the ministry of the Church in Jerusalem along with the Twelve. They preach, baptize, and bear witness to Jesus.

One of the seven, Stephen, preached to the Sanhedrin—the group of seventy Jewish religious leaders (see Nu 11:16) who had demanded that

---

30 Ac 6:6; see also Martin Chemnitz, *Ministry, Word, and Sacraments: An Enchiridion*, trans. Luther Poellot (St. Louis: Concordia Publishing House, 1981), 34–37.

Pilate have Jesus crucified (see Jn 19:6). Like Jesus, Stephen had been falsely accused of both blaspheming Moses and God and trying to destroy the temple (see Ac 6:11, 14). Some of the men who belonged to the synagogue of the Freedmen didn't like the signs and wonders he performed in Jesus' name. Consequently, they secretly instigated men to accuse him so that he could be arrested by the elders and scribes and brought before the Sanhedrin. When the high priest heard the accusations, he asked Stephen, "Are these things so?" (Ac 7:1).

Rather than replying with a simple yes or no, Stephen began by proclaiming God's promise of divine presence beginning with Abraham. He reminded the Sanhedrin of how God appeared to childless Abraham and promised that his offspring would inherit the Promised Land where he was currently sojourning, though after four hundred years of slavery. He spoke of how God even gave them a sign, the covenant of circumcision, as a guarantee of His promise. Then Stephen proclaimed how God faithfully fulfilled that promise by granting Abraham a son, Isaac, who underwent circumcision on the eighth day as God instructed. He recounted how God saved Isaac's son Jacob and his family from a famine in Egypt through Joseph. And how He saved the Israelites from four hundred years of Egyptian slavery through Moses. Stephen recited how God came down to dwell with the Israelites through the creation of the tabernacle and led them through the wilderness into the Promised Land.

While narrating God's faithfulness to His promise of divine presence throughout the Old Testament, Stephen simultaneously summarized Israel's response to it. They were jealous of Joseph, so they sold him into slavery. They rejected God's servant Moses by audaciously asking him, "Who made you a ruler and a judge?" (Ac 7:35). They turned away from God by idolatrously making and worshiping a golden calf. But then Stephen, looking at the Sanhedrin, added, "You stiff-necked people, uncircumcised in heart and ears, you always resist the Holy Spirit. As your fathers did, so do you" (Ac 7:51). And he proceeded to tell them how they sinned against God by betraying and murdering the fulfillment of His promise, Jesus, the Righteous One.

Rather than repenting of their sin, like those who heard a similar message proclaimed by Peter at Pentecost, the Sanhedrin angrily ground their teeth at him, stopped their ears, rushed at him, and dragged him out of the city. The false witnesses laid their garments down at the feet of a man named Saul and threw stones at Stephen. Yet all the while, Stephen, like Jesus, used his dying breath to pray for those who persecuted him. "Lord," Stephen cried, "do not hold this sin against them" (Ac 7:60).

That day marked the beginning of a great persecution for Christ's Church in Jerusalem. Saul, who had approved of Stephen's execution, went from house to house, searching for those who confessed the name of Jesus. As he identified the Christians, he would have them dragged off and locked in prison. The persecution was so intense that many Christians, except for the twelve apostles, fled Jerusalem to the region of Judea and Samaria, including the remaining six the apostles ordained (see Ac 8:1). And although scattered, the six continued to preach the word of Christ.

Hence Philip, the evangelist, traveled to Samaria preaching, teaching, casting out demons, and healing many who were paralyzed, all in the name of Jesus. Many who listened to Philip believed and were baptized, including a man named Simon who had previously practiced magic before coming to faith (see Ac 8:9–13). An angel of the Lord even directed Philip to travel on the road that leads from Jerusalem to Gaza. And the Holy Spirit then guided him to a chariot, where he met the treasurer of Queen Candace of Ethiopia (see Ac 8:27). At the time, the treasurer was reading a passage from the Book of Isaiah but didn't understand its meaning. Who was the man who was led like a sheep to slaughter, was silent, and had justice denied Him? the treasurer wondered (see Ac 8:31–34). Philip used this passage to proclaim Jesus, the Lamb of God who takes away the sin of the world. Upon hearing the Gospel, the treasurer wanted to be baptized. When they approached water, he commanded the chariot to stop. Philip baptized him and continued to preach the Gospel all the way from Azotus to Caesarea, about sixty miles (see Ac 8:40).

Thus, what began in Jerusalem now spread into Judea and Samaria. As Jesus' chosen instruments continued to bear witness about Him and administer the Means of Grace, He continued to make disciples from these nations, a people obtained by His own blood.

Meanwhile, back in Jerusalem, Christians were continually being imprisoned. Saul had appeared before the high priest and requested official letters so that he might travel all the way up to Damascus. His intent was to find Christians as he traveled and "bring them bound to Jerusalem"

(Ac 9:2). But our Lord Jesus Christ had other plans for him.

While he was on his way to Damascus, indeed as he approached the city, a light shone from heaven, Saul fell to the ground, and the voice of Jesus sounded, "Saul, Saul, why are you persecuting Me?" (Ac 9:4). Since Saul did not recognize who was speaking to him, nor did his traveling companions, Jesus proceeded to reveal Himself, saying, "I am Jesus, whom you are persecuting. But rise and enter the city, and you will be told what you are to do" (Ac 9:5–6). When Saul stood on his feet and opened his eyes, he suddenly realized he was blind. His traveling companions had to lead him by the hand into the city. But it was not the Lord's intention simply to stop Saul's persecution by leaving him in the dark. No. Saul had been living in the darkness of unbelief for far too long. Jesus wanted to take Saul and call him out of the darkness of sin, death, and the devil and into the marvelous light of His salvation.

Subsequently, Jesus spoke to Ananias, one of His disciples who was in Damascus, and told him to go to Straight Street, look for Saul from Tarsus, and lay hands on him so he could recover his sight (see Ac 9:11–12). At first, Ananias was reluctant, to say the least. After all, he had heard of the evil Saul had done in Jerusalem. And he knew that Saul came with the authority of the chief priests to imprison all who believed in Jesus. Nevertheless, Jesus assured Ananias that Saul had seen a vision where Ananias laid his hands on him, and he recovered his sight. Moreover, He told Ananias that Saul would be His chosen instrument. Through Saul, Jesus' name would be proclaimed not only to the children of Israel but also to the Gentiles and kings. And though Saul would suffer greatly for the sake of Jesus' name, he would inevitably count everything else as rubbish when compared to "the surpassing worth of knowing Christ Jesus" (Php 3:8).

Ananias believed the word of the Lord. He found Saul, laid his hands on him, and said, "Brother Saul, the Lord Jesus who appeared to you on the road by which you came has sent me so that you may regain your sight and be filled with the Holy Spirit" (Ac 9:17). At once, something like scales fell from his eyes. He recovered his sight and was baptized. But even more remarkably, Saul, who was later called Paul (see Ac 13:9), immediately entered the Damascus synagogue and proclaimed Jesus as the Christ and Son of God. Everyone who heard him preach was amazed. In truth, Paul was too. He marveled that Jesus chose to appear to him and call him into the Office of the Holy Ministry as an apostle. After all, Paul thought, "I am the least of the apostles, unworthy to be called an apostle, because I persecuted the church of God" (1Co 15:9).

Even so, Paul continued to preach to the Jews in the Damascus synagogue for many days. But the more Paul preached, the more confounded and angered they became. They were so irked by his preaching of Jesus as the Christ that they plotted to kill him. Thankfully, they never had the chance. Paul discovered their plot, and his friends helped him escape. They lowered him in a basket through an opening in the city wall under the darkness of night.

He had hoped to join the Twelve in Jerusalem, but they were afraid of him. However, Barnabas, a fellow believer in Christ, interceded for him. He brought Paul to the apostles. He recounted how Paul had personally spoken to Jesus on the road to Damascus and then boldly preached His name in the synagogue of Damascus. When the Twelve heard that Paul was now a believer and that Jesus had made him an apostle like them, they brought Paul to Caesarea. They would continue to preach the Gospel in Jerusalem, Judea, and Samaria so that the Church might continue to multiply. But Paul would be sent to his hometown, Tarsus, located in present-day Turkey, to begin to preach the Gospel to the Gentile nations so that God's message of salvation for all people in Jesus Christ might start to spread to the "ends of the earth" (Ac 1:8).

Paul's journey as Jesus' chosen instrument, or witness to the Gentiles, began in Tarsus, but it certainly didn't end there. While they were preaching the Gospel to both Jews and Gentiles in Judea and Samaria (see Ac 10:1–11:17), Peter and the other eleven heard that the Turkish city named Antioch had received the preaching of the Gospel. Consequently, they sent Barnabas to Antioch to investigate. And when Barnabas saw that there were many who confessed the name of Jesus, he hurried to Tarsus to find Paul and bring him to Antioch. For an entire year, both Paul and Barnabas taught the assembly of believers, the Church in Antioch, the fullness of God's message of salvation in Jesus Christ. Their teaching and proclamation of Christ became so renowned that the Antiochians created a term or label for these believers. They called them Christians, meaning the ones belonging to Christ (see Ac 11:26).

From there, Paul was "sent out by the Holy Spirit" (Ac 13:4) to a variety of Gentile nations. Over the course of about twenty-three years, Paul traveled on missionary journeys to Cyprus, Iconium, Lystra, Derby, Perga, Syria, Silicia, Galatia, Philippi, Thessalonica, Berea, Athens, Corinth, Phrygia, Ephesus, Macedonia, Athens, Crete, Troas, Miletus, and Rome, as well as other cities and regions.[31] And though he, like the Twelve, would suffer imprisonments, beatings, hunger, thirst, hardships, anxiety, and rejection for preaching Jesus Christ crucified and risen for the forgiveness of sins, Paul was not deterred (see 2Co 11:24–28). He was Jesus' chosen instrument to carry His name "before the Gentiles and kings and the children of Israel" (Ac 9:15). Thus, Paul preached. He preached Christ as "the power of God and the wisdom of God" (1Co 1:24). And the more Paul preached, the more Jesus continued to draw all people to Himself (see Jn 12:32). The more people Jesus drew to Himself, the more men He called into the Office of the Holy Ministry to care for the Church of God in those cities or regions. These men, though called by a variety of titles—"overseer" (Ac 20:28; 1Tm 3:2), "elder" (Ac 20:17; Ti 1:5), "shepherd" (pastor) (Eph 4:11), "minister" (Eph 3:7; Col 1:7)—were the resident clergy keeping watch over the local flock or Church, of which the Holy Spirit made them overseers. They administered the Means of Grace—Christ's Word, Holy Absolution, Holy Baptism, and Holy Communion—in a particular place while Paul continued to preach the Gospel as he traveled.

Yet whether it was these men, Paul, the six, or the Twelve, wherever the Word of Christ was purely preached and the Sacraments administered according to Jesus' command, there Christ abided as He promised. There, Jesus was present, calling and gathering a people for His own possession, a holy nation, a royal priesthood, the Church, which "He obtained with His own blood" (Ac 20:28). The Church, both pastor and people, which He created/formed by the Spirit, as well as by the water and blood that flowed from His pierced side (see 1 Jn 5:6–9; Jn 3:5–6). The Church, who is inseparably joined to Jesus, her Bridegroom (see Rm 6:3–4; Col 2:11–14; Eph 5:25–27). She is bone of His bones and flesh of His flesh (see Gn 2:23). Hence, she is called Christian, for she was taken out of Christ. In Him, she lives, moves, and has her being (see Ac 17:28). And by Him, the Church will continue to be sustained until the resurrection of all flesh (see 1Co 1:8–9).

---

31 Andrew E. Steinmann, *From Abraham to Paul*, (St. Louis: Concordia Publishing House, 2011), 343–45.

Accordingly, the middle of God's great story of salvation in Jesus Christ, postascension and preresurrection, is not so murky after all. It's rather glorious and comforting. For even though we wander through the wilderness of sin, the vale of tears, the valley of sorrow and death in this life, we are not alone. Jesus has not abandoned us nor left us as orphans. He still comes to us, as He promised (see Jn 14:16–18; Mt 18:20). He comes veiled in the Means of Grace, hidden in Word, water, bread, and wine, so that by His Spirit (see Gal 4:6), He might continually draw all people unto Himself and reconcile them to the Father. Put differently, the Father sent the Son in the power of the Holy Spirit that by the Spirit, we may be united to the Son who reconciles us to the Father, that together we may be one in Christ (see Jn 16:13–16; 17:20).

CHAPTER 7

JOINED
TO CHRIST

With God's breathtakingly beautiful picture of divine presence now in focus, there is one particular piece of this puzzle that remains. You! Where do you, with all your joys, sorrows, social interactions, life experiences, successes, failures, talents, and dreams fit into God's story of salvation for all people in Jesus Christ?

This question might seem a bit foreign or strange to us since we are used to selfishly orienting everything in our lives around us. We are accustomed to asking questions such as these: "What do I like? What do I want? How does this make me feel? What will this person, possession, or accomplishment do for me? Does this relationship fulfill my wants, desires, and dreams? Does this job make me happy?" We are used to taking people, groups, activities, and the things of this world and asking, "How does this piece of the puzzle fit into my life?" But none of us should think of ourselves more highly than we ought (see Rm 12:3). For our lives "are a mist that appears for a little time and then vanishes" (Jas 4:14). The truth is, this puzzle existed long before you or I entered the picture. Our lives are only one small part of a larger historical narrative. And they only find their true meaning, purpose, and worth when they are joined to it.

How then are you joined to God's story? Well, you might think that it's simply by virtue of being conceived and born into this world. And to a degree, you're right. You, like almost every human being before you, became part of God's story through the process of procreation that God designed and blessed Adam and Eve with back in the Garden of Eden (see Gn 1:28). Through one man and one woman, your father and mother, God fearfully and wonderfully made you (see Ps 139:13–14). He intricately formed your body and soul, eyes, ears, limbs, reason, and senses.[32] Moreover, He even knows the number of hairs on your head (see Lk 12:7). Succinctly put, you are an integral part of God's creation.

But being part of God's creation also means that you, like Adam and Eve, are corrupted with sin (see Rm 5:12; 1Tm 2:14). Out of your heart comes "evil thoughts, sexual immorality, theft, murder, adultery, coveting, wickedness, deceit, sensuality, envy, slander, pride, foolishness" (Mk 7:21–22). Daily, you fail to love both God and your neighbor. You, together with the rest of mankind, are by nature a child of wrath (see Eph 2:3). The wages of our sin is death, both the physical or temporal punishment

---

32 Small Catechism, First Article

where the heart stops beating and the lungs stop drawing breath, and the eternal punishment, a separation from the holy and perfect God. Hence, not one of us, when we were born and just able to talk, said, "Oh God? Let me tell you about God. He is the Father, the Son, and the Holy Spirit—three distinct persons, yet at the same time, only one God. And the Second Person of the Trinity, the Son, has two natures. He is simultaneously God and man . . . ." No. You, I, and the rest of humanity are dead in our trespasses and sins (see Eph 2:1). By nature, we do not know, understand, or seek God. We are far off and separated from Him.

As you know, however, God does not delight "in the death of the wicked" (Ezk 18:23). So out of love for His fallen creation, "God sent forth His Son, born of woman, born under the law, to redeem those who were under the law" (Gal 4:4–5). Jesus came for sinners. He "came to seek and save the lost" (Lk 19:10). And that includes you! Jesus came to redeem you, "not with perishable things such as silver or gold, but with the precious blood of Christ" (1Pt 1:18–19), which He shed for you, as He did for the world, on the cross. In this sacrificial act of love, Jesus atoned for the sins of the whole world, even yours (see 1Jn 2:2). He gave His life unto death and rose from the grave so that you "may be His own and live under Him in His kingdom."[33] In other words, while the wages of sin may indeed be death, the gift of God is eternal life, but only for those who are in Christ Jesus (see Rm 6:23).

The sad reality is that though everyone is created by God and Jesus died for all people, not everyone will receive eternal life. As previously stated in chapter 5, when Jesus returns, only those who believe in Him will hear those blissful words, "Come, you who are blessed by My Father, inherit the kingdom prepared for you from the foundation of the world" (Mt 25:34). Only those who believe in Him will be raised to eternal life with God (see Jn 3:16; 6:40; Rv 21:3–4). Everyone else, unbelievers, will rise to be condemned (Jn 5:29; Mk 16:16). Jesus alone is "the way, the truth, and the life" (Jn 14:6). "There is salvation in no one else, for there is no other name under heaven given among men by which we must be saved" (Ac 4:12). Consequently, apart from Christ, you are still a slave to sin, dead in your trespasses, separated from God, and thus lost and condemned forever. But if you are united to Jesus, if you are in Christ, you

---

33 Small Catechism, Second Article

are a new creation, a son of God, a temple of the Holy Spirit, and an heir of eternal life with Him (see 2Co 5:17; Gal 3:26–4:7; 1Co 6:19; Rm 8:17).

How can you become united to Jesus and therefore be in Christ? This is the work of the Holy Spirit. It is the Spirit who comes in Jesus' name (see Jn 14:26). The Spirit takes Jesus' victory of the cross and empty tomb, forgiveness of sins and eternal life, and declares it to you (see Jn 16:14). The Spirit pours the love of God into your heart (see Rm 5:5). The Spirit alone enables you to confess that "Jesus is Lord" (1Co 12:3). He accomplishes all of this in you by using the same powerful, tangible, everyday tools the disciples were equipped with. Today, as He has throughout the centuries, the Holy Spirit uses the Means of Grace to join you to and keep you in Christ.

The first means that the Spirit uses to join you to Jesus involves your ears. "Faith comes from hearing, and hearing through the word of Christ," Paul says (Rm 10:17). And that Word of Christ comes to us in two distinct ways: written and oral.

The written Word, which is also called "the Bible," "Holy Scripture," and "God's Word," is a collection of sixty-six books composed by over thirty authors over several thousand years. It is divided into two definitive sections of time. The Old Testament spans from the creation of the world to about four hundred years before Jesus' birth: from Genesis to Malachi. The New Testament spans from a few months before Jesus' birth to Jesus' return at the resurrection of all flesh: from Matthew to Revelation. And though there are two divisions of time, there remains only one intricate, breathtakingly beautiful narrative whose focus is divine presence. Hence after the creation of the world, mankind's fall into sin, and the resulting separation from God's presence, the rest of the Old Testament is spent looking for the Promised Child who will crush the head of the serpent and restore to us the presence of God. The New Testament is spent proclaiming that the Promised Child, Jesus, has come to restore to us the presence of God so that we may once again have eternal life with our eternal Lord. Simply put, the Bible is all about Jesus! It is the written account of God's story of salvation for all people in Jesus Christ.

This is what Jesus Himself told the Jews who were seeking to kill Him because they did not believe He was the Christ. To them, Jesus said, "You search the Scriptures because you think that in them you have eternal life;

and it is they that bear witness about Me" (Jn 5:39). Jesus also explained this to Cleopas and the other disciple on the road to Emmaus when He, beginning with Moses and the prophets, "interpreted to them in all the Scriptures the things concerning Himself" (Lk 24:27).

Since the Bible solely testifies to Jesus, the Word made flesh, who is the way, the truth, and the life, it is trustworthy and true, without error. "All Scripture is breathed out by God" (2Tm 3:16). And "no prophecy was ever produced by the will of man, but men spoke from God as they were carried along by the Holy Spirit" (2Pt 1:21). The Holy Spirit accurately brought to each authors' memory all that they had seen and heard concerning Christ. The authors faithfully recorded it in their own words and language so that "you may believe that Jesus is the Christ, the Son of God, and that by believing you may have life in His name" (Jn 20:31).

Similarly, the oral or preached Word is all about Jesus. As we have seen, when Adam, Abraham, Isaac, Jacob, Moses, Elijah, Isaiah, Jeremiah, Ezekiel, or one of the other patriarchs and prophets spoke, they spoke of the Promised Child who was coming to crush the head of the serpent and restore the presence of God. When Peter, John, Stephen, Philip the evangelist, Paul, or one of the other apostles or pastors spoke, they spoke of the Promised Child who has come to restore to us the presence of God. Irrespective of who God's chosen instrument was, all bore witness to what they had seen, heard, and received from God. They all preached Christ crucified: the power and wisdom of God for the salvation of everyone who believes (see 1Co 1:23–24; Rm 1:16). As they did, the Holy Spirit called people to faith in Jesus Christ (see 2Th 2:14).

Even today, the Holy Spirit calls people through that same powerful word, the Gospel. As the word of Christ enters your eyes or resonates in your ears, the Holy Spirit takes this, His sharp, living, active, two-edged sword, and cuts you to the heart, as He did at Pentecost, so that all your sinful thoughts, words, and actions, are now exposed (see Heb 4:12–13; Eph 6:17). What you once had not seen, you now see clearly. You are not perfect as your heavenly Father is perfect. Even your best works are but a polluted garment in the eyes of God (see Is 64:6). Through the reading and preaching of God's Law, as recorded in Holy Scripture, has come the knowledge of your sin (Rm 7:7). And you, like the tax collector, are led to cry out, "God, be merciful to me, a sinner!" (Lk 18:13).

Yet at the same time, the Spirit uses His sword to surgically remove your heart of stone and give you a heart of flesh (see Ezk 36:26). He gives you a new heart, a pure heart, one that has been "sprinkled clean" (Heb 10:22; see 1Pt 1:22–23). He implants the word of Christ in you, a word that creates faith (see Jas 1:21). He opens your mouth so that you might confess Jesus as Lord (see 1Co 12:3; Rm 10:9). By faith, you are justified or declared righteous, holy in His sight. You have peace with God and are saved by His grace (see Eph 2:8–9). You have been born again, not by the perishable seed of man but "through the living and abiding word of God" (1Pt 1:23).

The second means that the Spirit uses to join you to Jesus not only includes the Word of God, faith, and salvation but also is specifically focused on being born again and intimately tied to water. "Truly, truly, I say to you, unless one is born again . . . of water and the Spirit, he cannot enter the kingdom of God" (Jn 3:3, 5), Jesus tells Nicodemus. "Whoever believes and is baptized will be saved" (Mk 16:16), He declares to the Eleven. And "Baptism, which corresponds to this [the flood], now saves you, not as a removal of dirt from the body but as an appeal to God for a good conscience, through the resurrection of Jesus Christ" (1Pt 3:21), Peter proclaims.

Baptism is as simple and complex as it looks and sounds. It is simple because you feel and see yourself being submerged in water or having it poured or sprinkled on you three times. And as the water touches your skin, you hear the words "I baptize you in the name of the Father and of the Son and of the Holy Spirit."[34] But it is complex because the moment you feel that water and hear the very triune name of God spoken over you, you "have died with Christ" (Rm 6:8). As Paul says, "We were buried therefore with Him by baptism into death, in order that, just as Christ was raised from the dead by the glory of the Father, we too might walk in newness of life" (Rm 6:4). In Baptism, you are crucified and raised with Christ. Jesus' death is now your death. Sin and death have no power or dominion over Him, so they have no power or dominion over you. You don't belong to them. You are no longer enslaved to them. You have been set free. You belong to Him. You are marked with the cross of Christ both on your forehead and heart. You are "dead to sin and alive to God in Christ Jesus" (Rm 6:11).

---

34 LSB, p. 270.

Moreover, in Baptism, you have "put on Christ" (Gal 3:27). God has clothed you in the garment of salvation. He has covered you with a robe of righteousness, a robe made white, or holy and pure, by the blood of Jesus, the Lamb of God who takes away the sin of the world (see Is 61:10; Rv 7:14). He has cleansed and purified you by "the washing of water with the word" (Eph 5:26). He has sent the Spirit of His Son into your heart so that you can confidently call God your "Abba! Father!" (Gal 4:6). For that is what He is. God is now your dear Father, and you are His dear child, since you have received the Spirit of adoption as a son (see Rom 8:15). As a son of God, an offspring of Abraham, you are an heir of God and coheir with Christ (see Gal 3:29–4:31; Rm 8:17). All that Jesus won for you on the cross and through the empty tomb, namely forgiveness of sin and eternal life with your eternal God—the Father, the Son, and the Holy Spirit—is now given and belongs to you. Your inheritance is God's promise of divine presence, and its guarantee is the Holy Spirit with which you were sealed and who now dwells in you (see Eph 1:13–14).

How exactly can the waters of Holy Baptism do these miraculous works of begetting and saving? It is because Jesus, the Word made flesh, who spoke to the sea and all was calm, to demons and they were cast out, to a dead man and he was raised, spoke also to His chosen instruments: "Go therefore and make disciples of all nations, baptizing them in the name of the Father and of the Son and of the Holy Spirit" (Mt 28:19). It is solely by the power of Jesus' Word. He speaks, and His Word does what it says.

Consequently, your Baptism was a death to your sinful, earthly life and flesh and a resurrection and incorporation into the life of Christ. In and through Baptism, "you have died, and your life is hidden with Christ in God. When Christ who is your life appears, then you also will appear with Him in glory" (Col 3:3–4). Put more simply, your new, eternal life, your life in Christ, began when you were baptized.

And to be sure, your life in Christ will be brought to completion in a moment, in the twinkling of an eye, at the sound of the trumpet (see 1Co 15:52), when Christ returns to raise your body out of the dust and ashes of death so that you may live with Him in eternity. But in the meantime, you, like numerous Christians before you, find yourself living neither in the beautiful beginning nor the triumphal end of God's story. Rather, as shown in Figure 10, you find yourself living in the middle, postascension and preresurrection of all flesh.

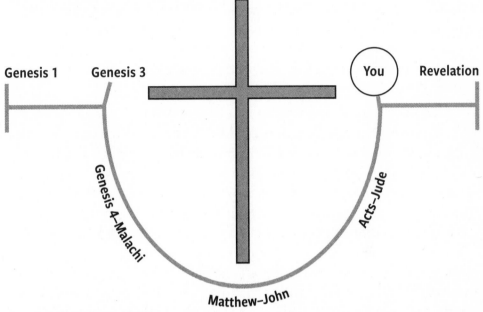

Figure 10: Living in the Middle

In the middle, Christ remains veiled from your eyes. You don't see Jesus face-to-face as you yearn and desire to. You don't see the new, imperishable, incorruptible, and eternal life that was given to you in the waters of Holy Baptism. Today, your life remains hidden with Christ in God. Like countless Christians before you, you are still surrounded by and face inconceivable amounts of pain and suffering: war, violence, hatred, divorce, suicide, rape, shootings, terrorism, theft, adultery, depression, anxiety, cancer, multiple sclerosis, amyotrophic lateral sclerosis (ALS), Parkinson's, Alzheimer's, dementia, natural disasters, the loss of a job or house, and the death of a spouse, child, grandchild, mother, father, sister, brother, family member, or friend. In the middle, you, like Paul, confess, "I do not understand my own actions. . . . For I do not do the good I want, but the evil I do not want is what I keep on doing" (Rm 7:15, 19). In the middle, the devil still "prowls around like a roaring lion, seeking someone to devour" (1Pt 5:8). And since you have been reconciled to God in Christ, the devil seeks to devour you. The devil is your adversary. You are in the world, not of the world (see Jn 17:16). For now, your life in Christ remains a daily battle against the devil, the world, and your own sinful flesh.

Often, the middle can feel like a lonely place. That's part of the devil's trick. He wants to isolate you. He wants you to feel the full weight of living in a world filled with sin, suffering, evil, pain, and death. He wants you to wonder: "Where are You, God? Don't You love me? Don't You care about me? Are You even real?" The goal of this isolation is to snatch you away from Christ.

But the reality is that you are not alone. Having been crucified with Christ, born again by the waters of Holy Baptism and the imperishable abiding Word of God, your body remains a temple for the Holy Spirit (see 1Co 6:19). Thus it is not simply you who live but Christ who lives in you (see Gal 2:20). He is your refuge, strength, and fortress (see Ps 91:2). And though you wrestle against "the cosmic powers over this present darkness, against the spiritual forces of evil" every day, it is the Lord who has and continues to clothe you with His garment of salvation, the whole armor of God: the belt of truth, the breastplate of righteousness, the Gospel of peace, the shield of faith, the helmet of salvation, and the sword of the Spirit (see Eph 6:11–17). Week after week, Sunday after Sunday, through the Means of Grace, Christ continues to adorn you in His victory and triumph so that you may stand firm in Him against the daily assaults and schemes of the devil.

Accordingly, when the devil attempts to entice you through the world or tempts you to indulge in the sinful desires of your heart, you can wield the shield of faith and the sword of the Spirit, the very Word of God, saying, "I refuse! I refuse to let the sins of sexual immorality, theft, murder, adultery, coveting, wickedness, deceit, sensuality, envy, slander, and pride reign in my mortal body. That is not who I am. I am not a slave to sin. I am a son of God. For I am marked with the cross of Christ on my forehead and heart. I was buried with Jesus in Baptism. I am dead to sin and alive to God in Christ Jesus. So 'Get behind me, Satan! For you are not setting your mind on the things of God, but on the things of man' (Mk 8:33)."

When you fail, when you fall into sin, the devil will attack you with his flaming arrows of accusations, saying, "How could you? How could you commit that atrocious sin? Children of God don't think, speak, or do that. No one in the world, not even God, could love you or forgive you after what you have done. It looks like you are more my child than God's child.

And we both know that in the end, my children will be cast out of the presence of God and into the fires of hell with me." However, when the devil's arrow of accusation strikes you, the breastplate of Christ's righteousness, the helmet of His salvation, and the belt of truth, given to you in Holy Baptism and Holy Absolution, protect you.

And standing firmly, confidently, and unharmed in Christ, you swing the sword of the Spirit saying two things. First, "I do not belong to sin, death, or even you, devil. I am a son of God. In Holy Baptism, God put His name on me (see Mt 28:19). He made me His son and clothed me in a robe of Christ's righteousness (see Gal 3:26–27). The blood of the Lamb covers all my sin (see Rv 7:14). I am holy, cleansed, and pure because Christ has washed me with His water and Word (see Eph 5:26–27)." Second, you confidently proclaim, "You are right, devil. I am a wretched man. But Jesus has saved me from this body of death (see Rm 7:24–25). He has said that if I confess my sins, He will forgive me and cleanse me from all unrighteousness (see 1Jn 1:9). Having confessed my sins, God has absolved me. Through the mouth of His chosen instrument, His pastor, God has said to me, 'I forgive you all your sins in the name of the Father and of the Son and of the Holy Spirit.'[35] So be gone, Satan. You have no power over me (see Mt 4:10)."

Moreover, when someone sins against you, when they hurt or harm you, the devil, the world, and your sinful flesh coax you to hold a grudge, retaliate, and get revenge. But the Gospel of peace with which your feet are shod tramples down and crushes Satan and his plans under your feet (see Rm 16:20). The Lord does not desire the death of a sinner, so neither do you (see Ezk 33:11). As Jesus loved and prayed for those who persecuted Him, so, too, do you. "Father, forgive them, for they know not what they do" (Lk 23:34; see Mt 5:44). A servant is not above his master (see Mt 10:24). As Christ has forgiven you, so also you forgive (see Col 3:13). You love because He first loved you by giving His life unto death (see 1Jn 4:10). And "love covers a multitude of sins" (1Pt 4:8).

Furthermore, when the fight is most fierce and the battle long, when inconceivable amounts of pain, suffering, and evil occur in your life, the devil does his worst. He utterly burdens you beyond your strength so that you, like Paul, might despair of life itself (see 2Co 1:8) and believe that

---

35 *LSB*, p. 185.

you are outside of God's care, outside of God's love, and are cast far from His presence. Or that you, like Job, might be encouraged to "Curse God and die" (Jb 2:9). But even in these moments, the Lord of Sabaoth, the general of the heavenly armies, Jesus Himself, is with you (see Ps 46:11; 91:11–12). He prepares a table before you in the presence of your enemies (see Ps 23:5) so that you might receive and bask in His triumphant victory over them.

He who veiled Himself in a burning bush now veils His body in the bread and His blood in the wine of Holy Communion (see Ex 3:2–4:17). The crucified and risen Christ who physically came to Thomas and the other disciples behind locked doors now physically comes to you (see Jn 20:19–23). He who fed and nourished His disciples on the shores of Tiberias after His resurrection now feeds and nourishes you (see Jn 21:4–14). He feeds and nourishes you, not with bread and fish but with His own body/bread and blood/wine. He does this so that you might participate, here and now, in the all-availing sacrifice of His body and blood given and shed for you on the cross at Golgotha and that you may taste and see that the Lord is good, that He is for you and not against you, angry at you, or looking to punish you. He loves you. He forgives you. He is with you even in the presence of your enemies.[36] Jesus is as close to you as the taste of the bread and wine in your mouth. And in eating and drinking Jesus' own body and blood, the shield of faith is renewed. Your heart is made brave, and your arms made strong once again. Because Christ has promised that "whoever feeds on My flesh and drinks My blood has eternal life, and I will raise him up on the last day" (Jn 6:54).

In these ways, through the Means of Grace, Christ continues to fight for you, with you, and in you. He's by your side upon the plain with His good gifts and Spirit,[37] enabling you to will and do according to His good pleasure (see Php 2:13). He does all of this so that you may be firmly and steadfastly kept in the one true faith, in Him alone.

What's more, Jesus also works in and through His people so that despite your daily battle, your life remains hidden with Christ in God. Regardless of how you may think or feel, your life in Christ is not lived in isolation nor in a bubble, as if it were only you and the triune God. The moment

---

36 FC SD VIII 79, 94.
37 *LSB* 656:4.

you die with Christ in Holy Baptism, you become part of the holy nation, the royal priesthood, the people whom Jesus obtained by the shedding of His precious blood. You become part of His body (see 1Co 12:13), the "one holy Christian and apostolic Church,"[38] which is comprised of countless people from every age, nation, tribe, and language, stretching all the way back to Adam and all the way forward to the resurrection of all flesh (see Rv 7:9).

And though Christ's body has many individual members, each with their own historical era, life experiences, social interactions, joys, sorrows, successes, failures, talents, abilities, and dreams, still you, with them, are one body with one Spirit, one Lord, one faith, one Baptism, and one God and Father of us all (see Eph 4:4–5). King David's Lord is your Lord (see Mt 22:44). Abraham, Isaac, and Jacob's God is your God (Ac 3:13). And since "He is not God of the dead, but of the living" (Mt 22:32) and Jesus is "the resurrection and the life" (Jn 11:25), you are surrounded by a great cloud of witnesses, both past and present—those who continually urge you to look to and rely on Jesus, "the founder and perfecter of our faith, who for the joy that was set before Him endured the cross . . . so that you may not grow weary or fainthearted" (Heb 12:1–3).

With God's peace dwelling richly in our hearts, we, the Church, instruct, comfort, forgive, care for, guide, and encourage one another with the Word of Christ through the singing of psalms, hymns, and spiritual songs (see Col 3:15–17). Your sorrows become our sorrows, as ours become yours. And your joys become our joys, as ours become yours. Hence "if one member suffers, all suffer together; if one member is honored, all rejoice together" (1Co 12:26). Together, we offer the living sacrifices of our bodies, time, skills, abilities, and financial resources through Jesus Christ (see 1Pt 2:5; Rm 12:1).

That is why when you are celebrating a birthday, Baptism, graduation, confirmation, pregnancy, the birth of a child, or anniversary or anxiously waiting for test results, battling an illness, dealing with the loss of a job, encountering a tragedy, enduring a natural disaster, or mourning the death of a loved one, your fellow saints[39] pray for you. In the face of joy, they

---

38 *LSB*, p. 158.
39 The term *saints* in Scripture refers to those who believe in Jesus and are thus made holy by His blood. See Col 1:2; Eph 1:1; and Rm 1:7.

donate money and set aside their busy schedules to attend or throw you a party, make you a quilt, bring you food, and rejoice with you that the steadfast love of the Lord endures forever (see Ps 118:1). In the face of sorrow, they take time to visit you in your hospital room, come to your home, call you on the phone, or send a card to remind you that God has not forgotten you, forsaken you, or abandoned you. He has engraved your name on the palms of His crucified and risen hands (see Is 49:14–16). In the face of death, they hold Christ before your eyes by proclaiming that Jesus is the resurrection, and whoever believes in Him shall live, even though they die (see Jn 11:25–26). Death cannot end our gladness, for we are baptized in Christ.[40] Finally, in all of these circumstances, God's chosen instrument, your pastor, comes to give you Jesus by reading His Word and administering Holy Communion.

Through the Church's genuine love for you and bold proclamation of Jesus to you, the Body of Christ aids you in wielding the shield of faith, swinging the sword of the Spirit, and standing firmly and confidently in Christ alone. That way, you, together with them, may continue to grow up into Christ, who is the Head, endure until the end, and obtain the outcome of your faith, the salvation of your body and soul (see Eph 4:15; 1Pt 1:9).

Your life then is not random, isolated, or independent. By virtue of your Baptism, you are inseparably joined to Jesus. You are connected to His body, a member of it. You are part of His Bride, the Church. You are bone of His bone and flesh of His flesh. You, like countless people throughout the ages, are called a Christian because you, like them, were created out of the water and blood that flowed from Christ's pierced side. Your life is one vital piece of God's larger historical narrative. It is firmly situated in the middle, postascension and preresurrection of all flesh. And though the darkness continues to deepen, Christ promises to abide with you and for you. And nowhere does that happen more regularly than in the Church's weekly gathering, in the Divine Service, where the Means of Grace, and Word and Sacraments are administered.

---

40 *LSB* 594:5.

CHAPTER 8

ABIDING
WITH CHRIST

Perhaps the words *Divine Service* seem rather odd and unfamiliar to you. That's not surprising since numerous Christians are accustomed to referring to the Church's weekly gathering as *worship*. We talk about going to church to worship God, grow in our faith, strengthen our marriages and families, find our purpose and meaning, become a better person, feel closer to God, and be comforted and uplifted by the format, music, and instrumentation of worship we think is best. To think of the Church's weekly gathering this way is to ask the question "How does this piece of the puzzle, the weekly church service, fit into my life?" In asking this question, you knowingly or unknowingly orient the Church's weekly gathering around your life. But again, none of us should think of ourselves more highly than we ought (see Rm 12:3). Even your life is not your own. You were bought at a price (see 1Co 6:20), not with gold or silver but the precious blood of Jesus (see 1Pt 1:18–19).

Just as your life does not belong to you, neither does the Church. The Church belongs to Jesus. He obtained it with His own blood. And you have been made an individual member of it. You are one of countless people from every age, nation, tribe, and language who live, move, and have their being in Christ (see Ac 17:28).

The Church's weekly gathering then is not primarily about the praises you sing to God, nor is it primarily about your faith, marriage, family, expectations, desires, or preferences, though they are certainly a small part of it. The weekly gathering is all about divine presence, God in the midst of His people. For Jesus, our Head, has promised that "where two or three are gathered in My name, there am I among them" (Mt 18:20).

And throughout the centuries, God's people have been confidently drawing near to Him that they may first and foremost "receive mercy and find grace to help in time of need" (Heb 4:16). We have been devoting ourselves to "the apostles' teaching and the fellowship, to the breaking of bread and the prayers" (Ac 2:42). We have been gathering in the name of Jesus to hear His merciful Word and receive His gifts of Baptism, Absolution, and the Lord's Supper, which have the promise of His presence and grace attached to them.[41] In essence, we have been gathering together chiefly to dwell with Christ and receive from Him, who is our great High Priest, the fruits of His all-availing sacrifice (see Heb 10:11–14).

---

41 Ap XIII 3–4

Only once we have received the fruits of His cross by faith does the whole Church in heaven and on earth erupt in endless joy and worship. Having received God's mercy, together with "angels and archangels and all the company of heaven we laud and magnify [His] glorious name."[42] By the Spirit, the one holy Christian and apostolic Church offers a sacrifice of thanksgiving (see Ps 116:17) to God in and through Christ, our intercessor (see 1Pt 2:5).

Thus, the Church's weekly gathering is rightly called the Divine Service.[43] For He who ascended to the Father's right hand now comes in the midst of His people to serve us with His gifts of salvation.[44] Jesus is present through His Word and Spirit, creating, redeeming, and sanctifying His people so that together we might continually be made holy, remain reconciled to the Father, and then offer a sacrifice of praise to God through Him.

There is an inherent majestic beauty when the Church gathers in church for the Divine Service. You enter a particular church building, located in a particular area, to gather with a particular people, in a particular time, for a particular service. But the moment the Divine Service begins, those boundaries begin to melt away. Suddenly, you find that your little assembly of people has entered the Most Holy Place through the veil of Jesus' flesh (see Heb 10:21–22). You have come to Mount Zion, to the city of God, to the heavenly Jerusalem, where all the citizens of heaven, those whose names are written in the Book of Life, are bound together as one (see Heb 12:22–24). It is no longer your little assembly; rather, your assembly is joined to the much larger assembly that consists of countless angels, with all the churches throughout the world, and those who have died in the faith and are with Jesus. Here, in this moment in time, in this weekly gathering, heaven and earth are inseparably joined as one. The Divine Service splices you into the triumphal end of God's story of salvation for us in Jesus Christ.[45] And all that is seen, heard, touched, tasted, and smelled proclaims this truth and allows you to live this story, this heavenly reality. The Divine Service gives you a foretaste of the coming heavenly feast (see Is 25:6).

---

42 *LSB Altar Book*, p. 225.

43 Historically, it has also been called the liturgy. See Ap XXIV 78–88, 232–34, as well as Fred L. Precht, *Lutheran Worship: History and Practice* (St. Louis: Concordia Publishing House, 1993), 58–62.

44 *LSB*, p. viii.

45 Arthur A. Just, *Heaven on Earth: The Gifts of Christ in the Divine Service* (St. Louis: Concordia Publishing House, 2008), 273.

The service begins the same way that your life in Christ began, with the sign of the cross and the name of the triune God. Both were given and placed upon you in Holy Baptism, where you became a child of God and were incorporated into the larger biblical narrative. And now, as children of God, you and your fellow saints boldly and confidently call upon or invoke His name. "In the name of the Father and of the Son and of the Holy Spirit,"[46] we cry out, trusting that He will hear, answer, and be present among us as He has promised (see 1Jn 5:14–15; Dt 12:5; Mt 18:20). As we speak God's name, each Christian traces the cross on themselves[47] by taking the thumb, index finger, and middle finger of their right hand, pressing them together in the shape of a triangle, symbolizing the Holy Trinity. When God the Father's name is spoken, you touch your forehead. Since God the Son is at the right hand of the Father, your hand moves downward toward the center of your chest and across to your right shoulder, touching it when His name is spoken. Then your hand moves from the right shoulder to the left, touching it when God the Spirit's name is spoken, and back to the center of your chest.

Standing steadfastly by the Spirit in Christ, you now enter God's presence through Jesus, your Mediator and High Priest. You draw near to the one true God in reverence and awe so that you may hear Him speak from heaven (see Heb 12:25, 28). However, upon entry into the Holy Place, you realize that you are "a man of unclean lips, and [you] dwell in the midst of a people of unclean lips" (Is 6:5). You are a "poor, miserable sinner"[48] whose eyes have seen God. And you know that sinners cannot stand in God's holy presence and live. Acknowledging your sin, you and the entire congregation kneel before God as beggars to confess.

> **Most merciful God, we confess that we are by nature sinful and unclean. We have sinned against You in thought, word, and deed, by what we have done and by what we have left undone. We have not loved You with our whole heart; we have not loved our neighbors as ourselves. We justly deserve Your present and eternal punishment.**[49]

---

46 *LSB*, p. 184.

47 The sign of the cross is also made at the end of the Absolution, the confession of the Creed, and the dismissal spoken after receiving Holy Communion.

48 *LSB*, p. 184.

49 *LSB*, p. 151.

In essence, we affirm God's judgment on our sin. We admit that we have knowingly and unknowingly sinned in our corrupt nature. We are soiled with sin. We have broken the first three commandments, the First Table of the Law. And we have broken the Second Table of the Law, commandments four through ten as well. Consequently, we deserve every earthly and timebound consequence and punishment we receive from God through those He has placed in authority over us. And we deserve the eternal, timeless punishment of separation from God.

Yet since we have entered God's presence through our great High Priest, we trust that God will be slow to anger, abounding in steadfast love and forgive all our sins because of Jesus and His all-availing sacrifice (see Nu 14:18). So we plead for God's mercy, and He freely gives it to us for Christ's sake. God, the judge of all, speaks a judgment of righteousness and acquittal through His chosen instrument, His pastor: "I forgive you all your sins in the name of the Father and of the Son and of the Holy Spirit."[50] We are now fully prepared to join the entire "assembly of the firstborn who are enrolled in heaven" (Heb 12:23) and, with them, enter God's presence with thanksgiving (see Ps 95:2).

Now, when an important earthly leader, such as a president, prime minister, or monarch, visits and dwells with the people, there is typically a grand ceremony including crowds lining the aisles, festal music, and a procession. How much more when the great King, the Lord of heaven and earth, comes to dwell with His people?

Having been cleansed from sin, the entire congregation stands out of respect for our God and King. The processional cross of Christ is lifted up and our eyes are firmly fixed on Him. Jesus leads us forth in peace to safely bring us to that heavenly Jerusalem, the Father's loving embrace. And we, His people, break forth into songs of praise—psalms, hymns, and spiritual songs (see Col 3:16)—which all proclaim the wondrous works of our God and extol His holy name. As the cross of Christ passes us, we, like the ten lepers and blind Bartimaeus, cry out, "Lord, have mercy upon us."[51] When the cross and God's chosen instrument, the pastor, approach the altar, our prayers for mercy and peace reach their ultimate expression. Heaven is now on earth. God is dwelling safely with His people. And with

---

50 *LSB*, p. 185.
51 See Mk 10:46–47; *LSB*, p. 186.

Jesus seated at the "right hand of the Majesty on high" (Heb 1:3), the entire assembly erupts into the hymn of incarnation or triumphal victory.

The *hymn of incarnation,* or Gloria in Excelsis, is the song of both the angels at Jesus' birth and a multitude of His disciples as He rides into Jerusalem on Palm Sunday (see Lk 2:14; 19:38). We join them in proclaiming that God, the eternal Word, the only Son of the Father, became flesh. We also join our voice with John the Baptist and confess that He became flesh to be "the Lamb of God, who takes away the sin of the world" (Jn 1:29). We declare with Stephen, Paul[52], and Peter that Jesus is at the right hand of God (see Ac 7:56; Heb 1:3; 1Pt 3:22). And by the Spirit, we again ask Him to "receive our prayer" and "have mercy on us."[53]

The *hymn of triumphal victory,* or "This Is the Feast," is the song of the twenty-four elders, the four living creatures, thousands of angels, and all creation in heaven at the resurrection of all flesh (see Rv. 5:12–13; 19:5–9). We join Adam, Abraham, Isaac, Jacob, Moses, Elijah, Isaiah, Jeremiah, Ezekiel, and all of Israel, who waited for the serpent's head to be crushed so that they may be set free from sin, death, and the devil and be restored to God's presence. But we also join Mary Magdalene, Peter, John, Mary the mother of Jesus, all who witnessed the resurrection, and everyone who has celebrated, is celebrating, or will celebrate the head-crushing blow delivered by Jesus, our Passover Lamb, as His blood was smeared on the post and lintel of the cross. Together, as the assembly of the firstborn in heaven, we rejoice that the serpent's head is forever crushed. Satan's reign is over. Sin and death are no more. And we, God's people, are finally, completely, and permanently free to enter His eternal, unveiled presence to eat and drink with Him at the marriage feast of Jesus, our Bridegroom and Lamb.

As Boaz spoke to the Bethlehem harvesters, the Angel of the Lord to Gideon, and Gabriel to Mary, so now the pastor speaks that same greeting to you and your fellow saints (Ru 2:4; Jgs 6:12; Lk 1:28). "The Lord be with you," he says. "And also with you," the congregation responds.[54] This simple greeting proclaims the profound reality that God's gracious presence and favor abide with both pastor and people of His Church, enabling them to do the specific responsibilities He has given them to do. God is with the pastor so that the Word of Christ is faithfully read and preached.

---

52 Along with various Church Fathers, the author believes Paul was the author of the Book of Hebrews.
53 *LSB,* p. 188.
54 *LSB,* p. 156.

And God is with His people so that they correctly hear it, believe it, and receive from it the forgiveness of sins and eternal life that God freely gives them in Christ.

To that end, the pastor prays a specific prayer known as the Collect of the Day. This magnificent prayer joins the character and work of God to our greatest needs. It focuses on an aspect of the Word of Christ that is about to be read. It petitions, "Almighty God," "Heavenly Father," "Only Son," "King," "Promised Seed," "Lamb," "Second Adam," "True Israel," and "Holy Spirit" to do His work of "freeing," "saving," "rescuing," "preparing," "delivering," "defending," "giving," and "raising from death," so that we might "receive," "understand," "repent," "inherit," "be set free," "live in righteousness and purity," and "partake of His resurrection." The pastor, standing in the stead of Christ and by His command, presents the people's prayers by the Spirit, through the Son, to the Father, so that whatever the petition, it may be "done for them by My Father in heaven" (Mt 18:19).

God is not silent or slow to answer our petitions. He immediately answers by giving us His powerful, living, and active Word, whose substance is Jesus. Beginning with Moses and the prophets, we, like the Emmaus disciples, hear God's great story of salvation for us in Jesus Christ. We, like Ezekiel and the apostles, now feast on the Word come down from heaven, the bread of life (see Ezk 3:3; Jn 6:51). We, like Mary of Bethany, now get to sit at Jesus' feet and listen to Him speak (see Lk 10:39).

The word Jesus speaks is not arbitrary or generic but deliberate and focused. It is ordered around the narrative of Jesus' coming, birth, life, death, resurrection, ascension, and the delivery of the Gospel to all nations. Annually and cyclically, we live the first half of the Church Year focused on the life of Christ, while in the second half we focus on our life in Christ. Accordingly, each Sunday has three assigned readings, typically an Old Testament, Epistle, and Gospel reading taken from a lectionary or "[structured] list of appointed Scripture readings for the Sundays, festivals, and [specific] occasions of the Church Year."[55] While these readings occur in three distinct eras of history, they all connect to, hold together, and culminate in Christ.

When we hear the Old Testament reading, we thematically hear God speak of the mighty works of salvation He did for His people during the

---

55 *LSB*, p. xxv.

time of Moses and the prophets. With them, we eagerly and expectantly wait for God's Promised Child to arrive. When we hear the Epistle, we thematically hear God speak of the mighty works of salvation He has done in Jesus during the apostles' time and will do again when Jesus comes in glory. Together with the apostles and all Christians who live postascension and preresurrection of all flesh, we eagerly and expectantly wait for the Promised Child, Jesus, to return and take us to be with Him. In hearing Moses, the prophets, and the apostles, we have been made ready and are prepared to receive the coming Christ, whose sandals neither they nor us are worthy to untie (see Lk 3:16).

Suddenly, the hour for God's answer to our prayers has come. Jesus, the Word made flesh, comes to speak to us. And with exuberant joy, we stand and burst into shouts of acclamation, "Alleluia. Lord, to whom shall we go? You have the words of eternal life. Alleluia, Alleluia."[56] We recognize that there is no other place that Jesus has promised to be present and audibly speak to us than right here and now in the reading of His Word. So we rejoice that "today salvation has come to this house" (Lk 19:9). And then, like the ten virgins, we hear the cry of our Bridegroom's presence ring out (see Mt 25:6), "the Holy Gospel according to . . .," and we meet Him in faith, singing, "Glory to You, O Lord."[57]

As the Gospel is read, we hear God's chosen instrument, the pastor, trumpeting His words. But in these words, we recognize the voice of Jesus, our Good Shepherd, speaking to us (see Jn 10:27). If our greatest need in the Collect of the Day is being rescued from the perils of our sin,[58] our Savior speaks of how He rode into Jerusalem on a donkey to save us (see Lk 19:28–40). If it is being raised from death,[59] the Second Adam proclaims His triumphant victory over death in His glorious resurrection (see Lk 24:1–12). Whatever the need, Jesus thematically speaks of who He is and what He has done for us so that we can be confident that God is in our midst saving, rejoicing over, and quieting us with His love (see Zep 3:17). And in response, we glorify His Holy name saying, "Praise to You, O Christ."[60]

---

56 *LSB*, p. 156.
57 *LSB*, p. 157.
58 *LSB Altar Book*, p. 743.
59 *LSB Altar Book*, p. 786.
60 *LSB*, p. 157.

What's more, hearing the voice of the risen Christ causes us to sing to the Lord a new song, to bless His name, and to tell of His salvation through the Hymn of the Day (see Ps 96:1–2). And while every hymn thematically tells and narrates your life into God's story of salvation, this hymn is most vital. The Hymn of the Day binds the appointed readings for the day together, summarizing God's gracious activity for His people in our hour of dire need into one grand proclamation. It takes the living voice of Jesus that was heard moments before in the readings and places it on the assembly's lips so that as we sing it, His word may be firmly planted in our hearts and minds. More than that, through the singing of this hymn, as well as the liturgical music and other hymnody in the Divine Service, we actively participate in the life and work of Jesus here and now. "Today this Scripture has been fulfilled in your hearing" (Lk 4:21), Jesus says. And we, like Mary, the mother of our Lord, respond in a hymn of praise, victoriously declaring that the Mighty One "has done great things for me, and holy is His name" (Lk 1:49).

The depth and profundity of Jesus' work among us is now unfolded and preached to us. It is not preached in a generic, simple, or superficial way but intimately and concretely. The whole counsel of God is preached rightly, that is properly dividing Law and Gospel, so that we may see our lives in the context of God's story. Put differently, Christ, through the mouth of His pastor, weaves together the three sacred eras of history[61] so that we may see that the Promised Child, who has come in the flesh of Jesus to suffer, die, and on the third day rise again, is in our midst trampling down sin, death, and the devil. Christ is here bestowing the fruits of His cross. He is redeeming. He is saving. He is forgiving. He is cleansing. He is bestowing eternal life. Through this magnificent proclamation, Jesus is intricately weaving our lives into His breathtakingly beautiful tapestry, picture, or story of divine presence.

Instantly, we, like the Virgin Mary (see Lk 1:38, 46–55), the Canaanite woman (see Mt 15:25–27), the centurion (see Mt 8:8–10), and countless others who have heard God's Word, respond in faith. We speak of who God is and what He has done for us. Together, we proclaim the mighty works of God throughout the ages: from Genesis to Revelation.

---

61 The three eras of history are (1) an Old Testament narrative that shows a mighty act of God, (2) its fulfillment in the person and work of Jesus as recorded in the New Testament Gospel narrative, and (3) the current life of Christ's Church in the Divine Service.

And since time would fail to enumerate and articulate them all, we use the CliffsNotes or SparkNotes of the Christian faith. We join our voices with thousands of faithful Christians who, for nearly two millennia, have confessed their faith using the clear, concise, and summarized words of the Apostles', Nicene, and Athanasian Creeds. Through these words, we proclaim the ongoing activity of the one true God—Father, Son, and Holy Spirit—creating, redeeming, and sanctifying us.[62]

What happens next is something truly extraordinary. We who are many, who each have our own little world complete with our own family, friends, and community, now come together as one body for the sake and life of the entire world. All Christians bring the entirety of their lives with them into the assembly of the firstborn. You bring your individual sorrows, joys, worries, family, friends, city, state, and country as your fellow saints bring theirs. And together, we offer supplications, prayers, intercessions, and thanksgivings for all people (see 1Tm 2:1). We pray for the pure proclamation and reception of the Gospel in the Church and throughout the world. We pray for the governors and legislatures of every city, state, and province, as well as all presidents, monarchs, and world leaders. We pray for our life in the world, that it be peaceful, quiet, honest, and godly. We pray for those who are in "trouble, want, sickness, anguish of labor, peril of death, or any other adversity."[63] We pray that the world would be protected from natural disasters, war, bloodshed, violence, and famine. We pray for our schools, our armed forces, those who are hospitalized, as well as those celebrating birthdays and anniversaries. In this cosmic sacrificial act of love, the Church is in the world and not of the world making intercession for the entire world by the Spirit through the Son to the Father. And we trust that the Father will hear our prayer and grant it for the sake of Christ, as He has promised (see Mt 18:19).

Our timebound yet timeless dwelling with God in the Divine Service now takes a glorious turn. The presence of Christ that first came to us through hearing now comes to us bodily in eating and drinking.[64] We who heard the voice of Jesus, our Good Shepherd, are now led by Him so that we may feast on His body and blood, at His table, in His presence.

---

62 LC II 7.
63 *LSB Altar Book*, p. 440.
64 Just, *Heaven on Earth*, 208.

As the Lord's Table is being set for the feast, we, God's royal priesthood, offer "a sacrifice of praise to God, that is, the fruit of lips that acknowledge His name" (Heb 13:15). Hearing the voice of our Good Shepherd and seeing His table set before our eyes causes us to sing of how God is at work creating a clean heart and renewing a right spirit within us so that we may enter into His presence and receive the joy of our salvation.[65] It produces deep reverence and awe in us as we see the love and mercy God has for us sinners in Christ's suffering, death, and resurrection (see Ps 116:12; 1Tm 1:15). It makes us hunger and thirst for Christ's righteousness (see Mt 5:6) so that we take God's cup of salvation offered to us in Holy Communion,[66] receive it with joy, and be satisfied in the fullness of His presence. It generates an outpouring of love for God and neighbor that expresses itself in the generous and cheerful giving of monetary gifts, which the Lord first gave to us, that will now be used for the proclamation of His eternal Gospel in the Church and throughout the world.

With the banquet prepared, the Lord sends His chosen instrument with an invitation, an announcement of His presence, and a call to come to His Son's wedding feast (see Mt 22:1–3). "The Lord be with you. . . . Lift up your hearts."[67] Simultaneously, God says to us who are last and lowest in His kingdom, "Friend, move up higher" (Lk 14:10). And clothed in our wedding garments, the baptismal robe of Christ's righteousness,[68] we, with all the faithful, enter the Most Holy Place, the heavenly marriage feast of the Lamb, with thanksgiving.[69] Together "with angels and archangels and with all the company of heaven, we laud and magnify"[70] God's glorious name. Our voices ring with the angelic multitude in the heavenly courts of the Most Holy Place in the Old Testament temple. "Holy, holy, holy Lord God of Sabaoth, heav'n and earth are full of Thy glory."[71] Yet at the same time, they resound with the crowd of disciples who greeted Jesus with shouts of "Hosanna" as He triumphantly rode into Jerusalem to offer Himself as the Lamb of sacrifice to atone for the sins of the world. In this moment, we recognize that nowhere is God's name more

---

65   Ps 51:10; *LSB*, pp. 192–93.
66   *LSB*, pp. 158–59; Mt 26:27.
67   *LSB*, p. 194.
68   *LSB*, p. 271.
69   *LSB*, p. 161.
70   *LSB Altar Book*, p. 241.
71   *LSB*, p. 195.

glorious and glorified than at the hour of Jesus' death (see Jn 12:27–32; 13:31–35; 17:1–5).

But before we gather at the Lord's Table to celebrate, remember, and proclaim Jesus' death by eating and drinking this heavenly feast, we first pray together the prayer our Lord Jesus taught us to pray (see Mt 6:9–13; Lk 11:1–4). In the Lord's Prayer, we, God's children, ask our dear Father to give us a whole host of things, including the purity of His Word, a godly life, faith created and strengthened by the Holy Spirit, everything needed to sustain our body and life, the forgiveness of sins, protection from the devil's assaults, a blessed death, and eternal life. However, when we pray the Lord's Prayer before we partake of the Lord's Supper, we eagerly anticipate God's emphatic "Yes! Here is My Son, Jesus. Here is the bread of life. Eat His body. Drink His blood. Receive everything you need for your body and soul. Live with Me forever, in My kingdom, which never ends."

And with that, the bread and wine are lifted before our eyes and the words of Christ echo in our ears. "Take, eat; this is My body. . . . Drink of it, all of you, for this is My blood of the covenant, which is poured out for many for the forgiveness of sins" (Mt 26:26–28; see also 1Co 11:23–25). This is no ordinary feast. This is no ordinary food. This is a foretaste of the eternal heavenly feast to come. This is the Holy Supper of Jesus' own body and blood.[72] This is Nazareth, Bethlehem, Golgotha, Easter, Pentecost, ascension, and eternity all given to us in a moment in time. This is heaven come down to earth. This is the crucified, risen, ascended, and reigning Christ, here and now for you.

Peace is on earth once again. His name is Jesus Christ, Son of God. He who offered Himself as the Lamb of God to take away the sins of the world comes to have mercy on us and give us His peace (see Jn 1:29). He comes to sprinkle His blood of the new covenant on our hearts (see Heb 9:12–14; 10:19–22; 12:24), that the temple of our bodies (see 1Co 6:19) might continually be cleansed from sin, inside and out. Hence, we sing, "O Christ, Thou Lamb of God, that takest away the sin of the world, have mercy on us . . . grant us Thy peace."[73]

In reverence and humility, we now intimately draw near to God to receive the marriage feast of rich food and well-aged wine (see Is 25:6).

---

72 *LSB*, p. 166.
73 *LSB*, p. 198.

Together, as the Body of Christ, we partake of the body and blood of Jesus Christ. As we all eat from the one bread and drink from the one cup, we actively receive, remember, and participate in the true body and blood of our Lord Jesus Christ given and shed for us on the cross at Golgotha (see 1Co 10:16–17; 11:24–25). More succinctly stated, the crucified and risen Christ is truly present as He delivers His very body and blood to us to eat and drink through the hand of His chosen instrument.

"How can this be?" some have wondered throughout history. But this is not a mystery that can be unraveled, explained, or fully comprehended by sin-corrupted human reason. These are the powerful, living, active words of Jesus to be received in faith. He has said, "Take, eat; this is My body. . . . Drink of it, all of you, for this is My blood" (Mt 26:26–28). So we do. In faith and unity of confession,[74] we eat and drink the precious gift of His body and blood, given in, with, and under the bread and wine. And they bestow the tremendous benefits of forgiveness of our sins, strengthening of our faith, and an intimate fellowship with Christ and one another, His Body, the Church.

The beauty, glory, and majesty of this profound reality is divulged in the song of our solemn assembly. We sing with Simeon, who held the Promised Child in the palms of his hands and declared,

Lord, now lettest Thou Thy servant depart in peace according to Thy word, for mine eyes have seen Thy salvation, which Thou hast prepared before the face of all people, a light to lighten the Gentiles and the glory of Thy people Israel.[75]

It is true, since we have received Jesus, that we, too, can now die in peace and joy. In fact, more than ever, we want to "depart and be with Christ" (Php 1:23) since it is far better than to remain in this wilderness of sin, this vale of tears, this valley of sorrow and death. Receiving this glimpse of God's glory, the foretaste of the coming heavenly feast, produces a deep desire within us. We, like Peter, want to cry out, "It is good that we are here" (Lk 9:33) and remain on this holy mountain.

But if we do not die right then and there, Jesus, our great High Priest,

---

74 See Appendix on p. 140 of this book.
75 *LSB*, pp. 199–200.

dismisses us with His priestly blessing. "The LORD bless you and keep you; the LORD make His face to shine upon you and be gracious to you; the LORD lift up His countenance upon you and give you peace."[76] For now, you, I, and the rest of the Church on earth leave Mount Zion, the heavenly Jerusalem, and are sent back into the world.

However, your descent back into the world, into your family, friends, and community, is not devoid of joy, purpose, or even the presence of God. Having dwelt with and received Christ in the Divine Service, you step out of the church doors and back into the world with an inexplicable joy. You have seen the glory of the only Son from the Father, Jesus, the true light of the world (see Jn 1:14; 8:12). The love of God has been poured into your heart through the Holy Spirit (see Rm 5:5), and Christ firmly dwells in you (see Eph 3:17). Whatever you do, in word or deed, you do "in the name of the Lord Jesus, giving thanks to God the Father through Him" (Col 3:17). And what you do, what Christ has sent you back into the world to do, is love one another as He has loved you (see Jn 13:34).

What does that look like? Well, it does not look like the world's conception of love. When the world speaks of love, it does so rather selfishly. You may hear a man and a woman say to each other, "I love you." When asked what they mean, answers of liking how they look, make me look or feel, encourage me, believe in me, help me, support me, inspire me, or are there for me abound. Similarly, when you hear someone say, "I love ice cream," they then talk about how ice cream makes them feel, how it tastes, smells, cools them off, and so on. But when Jesus speaks of love, He speaks of it as selfless action: "Greater love has no one than this, that someone lay down his life for his friends."[77] Love is about the giving of yourself for the sake of another. Love looks like sacrifice. Consequently, as God's people, His royal priesthood, we step out of the church doors and back into the world to offer ourselves as a living sacrifice in loving service to our neighbor. We engage in the good works God has prepared for us to do (see Eph 2:10).

If you are a husband, then you're busy daily offering the sacrifices of your wants, needs, time, strength, energy, even your very life, if need be, for the good of your wife. You are loving and cherishing your wife by thinking of and putting her before yourself (see Eph 5:25–29). If you are a

---

76 Nu 6:24–26; see also *LSB*, p. 202.
77 Jn 15:13; see also Jn 3:14–16; Lk 22:24–27; 1Jn 4:10; Eph 5:25; 1Co 13.

wife, then you are not only receiving the benefits of your husband's sacrificial offerings, but you are also offering your own sacrifices in response to and for the good of your husband (see Eph 5:22–24). You are putting his wants and needs before your own. You are giving your time, strength, and energy as you help him, speak well of him, and respect him.

If you are a parent, then you daily offer the sacrifices of time, patience, strength, money, knowledge, and discipline to "train up a child in the way he should go" (Pr 22:6). You are teaching your children about God's great love for them in Jesus Christ by bringing them to the Divine Service each week, reading the Bible to and praying with them throughout the day, singing hymns, and even praying one or more of the daily offices[78] or prayers out of the hymnal.[79] You are also working to provide a house, food, clothes, and an education for your child's well-being.

If you are a growing child, then you are not only dependent on your parents' sacrifices but you are also offering sacrifices of obedience to "honor your father and your mother" (Ex 20:12; see Eph 6:1–2). You are listening to their guidance and instruction. You are helping with chores around the house. You are addressing them kindly and showing that you value them highly.[80] As grown-up child, you honor your parents by sacrificing your body and possessions to help, serve, and provide for them when they are old, sick, infirm, or poor.[81]

Since you live in a particular city, state, and country, you offer the civil sacrifices God's governing authorities need and require (see Rm 13:1–7; 1Pt 2:13). You strive to be a good citizen. You pay taxes, obey ordinances and laws, vote, debate political issues, and show respect to and pray for all who are in authority over you (see 1Tm 2:2). You might serve in the armed forces or run for a local, state, or national political office. If the governing authorities establish a law that would cause you to sin, then you cannot. You "must obey God rather than men."[82] You might engage in lawful civic activism in order to change it. And you are willing to accept the punishment for disobeying it.

You may also be a grandparent, brother, sister, aunt, uncle, student,

---

78 For Matins, Morning Prayer, Evening Prayer, Vespers, and Compline, see *LSB*, pp. 219–59.
79 For Daily Prayer for Individuals and Families, see *LSB*, pp. 294–98.
80 LC I 107.
81 LC I 111; see also 1Tim 5:4.
82 Ac 5:29; see also AC XVI 7.

employee, or employer. In each of these vocations, these special relationships God has given to you, you offer yourself as a living sacrifice for the benefit of your neighbor. With a compassionate heart, kindness, humility, meekness, patience, and forgiveness, you love one another as God has loved you in Christ and as He has given you to do (see Col 3:12–14). And as you do, you also get the opportunity to proclaim the excellencies of Christ, who has called you out of darkness into the marvelous light of His salvation (see 1Pt 2:9). You get to tell your neighbor God's story of salvation for us in Jesus Christ.

The most remarkable part about all of this is that the sacrifices that are offered are not you but Christ who lives in you (see Gal 2:20). By the Spirit, through the reception of His Word and Sacraments, Christ dwells in your heart through faith (see Eph 3:17). God is at work in you to will and do His good pleasure (see Php 2:13). He uses your hands, feet, and mouth to speak for, feed, clothe, provide for, protect, and care for His creation. You serve as a mask of God.[83] In and through you, Christ abides for the sake and life of the world.

Even when you fail, even when you sin against God and your neighbor, He continues to work in you through His Word. God's Law runs through your mind or rings in your ear through the voice of the person you sinned against (see 2Sm 12; Mt 18:15; Rm 7:7–25). He calls you to repentance and faith. He makes you hunger and thirst for righteousness (see Mt 5:6). He drives you back to the foot of the cross, back to the Divine Service, so that you might "receive mercy and find grace to help in time of need" (Heb 4:16).

Christ's presence in your life is for more than one hour a week. He regularly and intimately abides with you in the Divine Service. He also abides in and with you every minute of every hour of every day out in the world. So, whether you are in Divine Service receiving the fruits of Christ's all-availing sacrifice and getting a glimpse of God's glory in the heavenly Jerusalem or out in the world serving as a mask of God, Jesus is with you. Here in time, your life always remains hidden with Christ in God (see Col 3:3). For you, as for all members of the Body of Christ, "to live is Christ," but "to die is gain" (Php 1:21).

---

83 See AE 14:114.

CHAPTER 9

LIVING
UNDER CHRIST

For you, as for all members of the Body of Christ, "to live is Christ," but "to die is gain" (Php 1:21). "A gain? How is death a gain?" you might wonder, even as a Christian. This is a fair and honest question since death brings such great loss: loss of status, possession, and people we love, including our grandma, grandpa, father, mother, child, sister, brother, aunt, uncle, family member, or friend. Death, the wages of our sin, looms over us. As it gradually approaches, it mocks us through gray hair, wrinkled faces, creaky knees, aching joints, canes, walkers, wheelchairs, and worn out bodies. As it rapidly approaches, it threatens to stop our heart, cease our breathing, and close our eyes. It tries to strike terror in our hearts as it calls to us, saying, "I'm it. I'm all you have to look forward to. I'll take you away from everyone you love and care about. And there is nothing that you, or anyone else for that matter, can do about it. There is nothing left for you but darkness, dirt, and decay." To be sure, death is a fierce and powerful enemy. Its mouth is always wide open, foaming, and salivating. It constantly rubs its hands together, clenches its fists, grits its teeth, and waits to pounce, consume, and swallow us whole.

But for all death's rage and terror, one crucial truth remains. There is one truth that death does not want to admit, nor does it want you to know, remember, or firmly believe. The truth is death is defeated. It tried to conceal, consume, and swallow Jesus' body whole, but it could not. He who joined us as dust was not reduced to dust and ashes. For when the women came to the tomb on Easter morning expecting to find death, they found life. When Peter and John peered into Jesus' tomb, they saw nothing except His grave cloths lying there and His face cloth folded neatly and placed to the side. The angels cried out, "Why do you seek the living among the dead? He is not here" (Lk 24:5–6). Mary proclaimed, "I have seen the Lord" (Jn 20:18). Cleopas spoke to Him. The disciples ate with Him. And Thomas touched His risen body. Jesus shattered the bonds of death when He burst forth from the tomb on Easter morning. The grave has been emptied of its power because Jesus lives. He is the resurrection and the life (see Jn 11:25).

Since you have died with Christ in the waters of Holy Baptism, death has no power over you either (see Rm 6:3–22). You do not belong to death. You belong to life. Yours is the victory through Jesus Christ our Lord (see 1Co 15:57). And nothing, not even death, can snatch you out of His crucified and risen hands (see Jn 10:28; Rm 8:38–39).

It will try. There will come a time when death rapidly approaches you, when your lungs cease to draw breath, your heart stops, and your eyelids are closed in death. There will come a time when your body and soul are separated by the cold hand of death. But when the time comes, you have nothing to fear. For even though you walk through the valley of the shadow of death, Jesus, your Good Shepherd, is with you (see Ps 23:4). His voice calls to you, "Truly, I say to you, today you will be with Me in paradise" (Lk 23:43). And His promise to you, and all believers in Him, remains: "I am the resurrection and the life. Whoever believes in Me, though he die, yet shall he live, and everyone who lives and believes in Me shall never die" (Jn 11:25–26).

Consequently, physical or temporal death is not the end of your story. True, your body and soul are separated. And your perishable body is sown, or buried, in the ground (see 1Co 15:36–37, 42). But your soul goes to be "away from the body and at home with the Lord" (2Co 5:8). Like Paul, you have fought the good fight, finished the race, and kept the faith (see 2Tm 4:7). And now you get to depart to "be with Christ" (Php 1:23) and rest from the labor of your daily battle against the devil, the world, and your own sinful flesh (see Rv 6:11; 14:13). This is a Christian's gain—your gain in the hour of death.

And though it is a joyous and blissful gain, it is not our full, final, lasting, and unbridled hope and joy. Indeed, it cannot be. Because when God created man, He didn't just breathe the breath of life. Rather, He breathed the breath of life into nostrils that He had created. He breathed the breath of life into man's body, which He formed from the dust of the ground (see Gn 2:7). And He took the time to knit you together, to form your body with all its parts, inside your mother's womb (see Ps 139:13–14). Your body is a vital aspect of who you are.

Just stop and think about it. What do you miss most about your family and friends who have died? Do you miss their smile? Do you miss their laugh? Do you miss the sound of their voice? How about the warm embrace of a hug? What about the smell of their soap, shampoo, cologne, or perfume? Is it the comfort and security of simply hearing them breathe or feeling them move as you lay next to them? Or is it the joy of sharing your everyday life with them, knowing that no matter what happens that day, they are with you, and you help, comfort, support, and care for one another? If the body matters that much to you and me, how much more does it matter to the Lord?

The separation of our body from our soul is so important that God the Son willingly assumed a body, took on flesh, and became man. Jesus redeemed our bodies by giving His body unto death on a cross. And while His body was taken down from the cross, carefully prepared for burial, and laid in the tomb, it did not remain there. God raised Him up from the dead (see Ac 2:32). What was sown perishable was raised imperishable (see 1Co 15:42). His natural or mortal body was raised spiritual or immortal (see 1Co 15:44; Lk 24:39). And because Jesus' body was raised from death, so shall your body be raised to immortality (see Rm 8:11). We believe in "the resurrection of the body, and the life everlasting."[84] "For as in Adam all die, so also in Christ shall all be made alive. But each in his own order: Christ the firstfruits, then at His coming those who belong to Christ" (1Co 15:22–23).

The resurrection of the body, the restoration of our soul to our body, and eternal life with our eternal Lord—when the trumpet sounds and Jesus returns in all His glory to take us to be with Him—is our full, final, lasting, and unbridled hope and joy. It is what the saints on earth long for as we cry out, "Come, Lord Jesus!" (Rv 22:20). It is also what the saints in heaven—those who died in Christ and are with Him now—desire as their souls cry out, "O Sovereign Lord, holy and true, how long before You will judge and avenge our blood on those who dwell on the earth?" (Rv 6:10). It is what Paul urges us Christians to comfort one another with as we mourn the death of fellow saints (see 1Th 4:15–18). It is what calms your fears while you lie on your deathbed. And it is what tempers the deep sorrow your family and friends feel as they stand in front of your casket and huddle at your graveside.

If you have ever been to a funeral service, then you know the feeling of deep sorrow—the wave of loss that rushes over you as you see your loved one's lifeless body a minute before their casket closes. The flood of memories and the feelings of loneliness that race through your mind in those brief but seemingly endless moments of silence as you wait for the service to begin or the next person to come and talk to you. The onslaught of anxiety and utter helplessness you experience as you walk toward the

---

84 Apostles' Creed in *LSB*, p. 159.

grave and watch the pallbearers place the casket on the lowering device. Any one of these moments, every one of these moments, is a poignant reminder that while our last enemy, death, is defeated, it has yet to be fully overcome and destroyed (see 1Co 15:26).

Though the war has been won and the victory is ours, the battle still rages on. Death ferociously lunges on those who mourn and sow in tears (see Ps 126:5). It wants nothing more than to shatter our shield of faith with its relentless attacks of sorrow, loneliness, helplessness, and endless despair. Yet onto this bleak battlefield rides He who is light and life. For us still fights the Valiant One, Jesus, our Sabaoth Lord, who holds the field forever.[85] He rides not in the clouds, at least not yet. No. For now, He rides humbly and victoriously in His Word, which is triumphantly trumpeted by His chosen instrument in the funeral and graveside committal services. He rides to give us true and lasting strength, hope, mercy, and comfort.

There is nothing truer, more permanent, stable, powerful, and comforting than God Himself. He is "the same yesterday and today and forever" (Heb 13:8). Thus the funeral service begins with the name of He who has power over death and the grave (see 1Sm 2:6; Jn 5:21). "In the name of the Father and of the Son and of the Holy Spirit,"[86] we confidently cry. For we believe and confess that while death changes so much of our life and the world here in time, it cannot change who we are. "Whether we live or whether we die, we are the Lord's" (Rm 14:8). The same cross, name, and white robe with which we were adorned in the waters of Holy Baptism still mark and cover us in the hour of our death.

The proclamation of this reality is most vividly shown in the "Remembrance of Baptism" when a white garment or pall is draped over the casket. It is typically embroidered with either a cross or the Chi-Rho symbol, which looks like a tall letter *P* with an *X* through it but is actually the first two Greek letters in the title Christ. Even now, we are "clothed with a robe of Christ's righteousness that covers all [our] sin."[87] "We have been united with Him in a

---

85 See *LSB* 656.
86 *LSB*, p. 278.
87 *LSB*, p. 278.

death like His, we shall certainly be united with Him in a resurrection like His" (Rm 6:5). Our life remains "hidden with Christ in God" (Col 3:3).

And He who led us in life now leads us in death. The processional cross of Christ is lifted up, and Jesus, our great High Priest, brings us safely to the Father once again. He leads us forth so that we may lie down and rest in peace and safety (see Ps 4:8). And through the singing of psalms, hymns, and spiritual songs, we, His people, comfort one another and remind one another that despite what we see and feel today, death is not forever and does not win. "Jesus lives! The vict'ry's won! Death no longer can appall me; Jesus lives! Death's reign is done! From the grave will Christ recall me. Brighter scenes will then commence; This shall be my confidence."[88]

If actions speak louder than words, then there are two actions that occur in this moment that boomingly thunder the reality of death's defeat and the confidence we have in the crucified and risen Christ. The first is the positioning of the casket. When the casket reaches the altar during the procession, it is placed before the altar at a perpendicular, or right angle.[89] In essence, the altar and the casket together form the shape of the cross and declare that this embodied instrument of death has now become God's instrument of life. The beacon of sorrow and despair has become the beacon of hope and joy. For on the cross "was hung the salvation of the world."[90] Jesus was high and lifted up on the altar of the cross to atone for the sins of the whole world, draw all people to Himself, and give them eternal life (see Jn 3:14–16; 6:40; 12:32–33). The cross is now "a life-giving tree for all who trust in Him."[91] Even in death, it bears the fruit of forgiveness, eternal life, and salvation.

The second action is the use and positioning of the paschal candle. This candle with its stand towers over the casket at roughly seven feet high. It symbolizes Jesus' "resurrection victory over the darkness of sin and death."[92] Accordingly, it is the prominent candle that is lit and displayed near the altar during the season of Easter, from the Vigil of Easter to Ascension Day.[93] It is also lit and placed next to the baptismal font during

---

88 *LSB* 490:1.
89 See *LSB Agenda*, p. 117.
90 *LSB Altar Book*, p. 517.
91 *LSB*, p. 209.
92 Lee A. Maxwell, *The Altar Guild Manual: Lutheran Service Book Edition*, (St. Louis: Concordia Publishing House, 2008), 46.
93 Maxwell, *The Altar Guild Manual*, 47.

the service of Baptism to announce that Jesus' victory is now our victory since we have just been buried and raised with Christ (see Rm 6:3–11). But when it is lit and placed near the head of the casket, the paschal candle proclaims that even in death, ours is the victory through Jesus Christ our Lord (1see Co 15:57). He will raise and transform our lowly, perishable body to be like His glorious, imperishable body (see Php 3:21).

And since faith comes by hearing, what was told through action is now proclaimed concretely in words. The trampling down of death and the resurrection of the body to eternal life with God are the substance of what is spoken, confessed, and heard in the funeral readings, the Creed, and the Hymn of the Day. Each one of these things recounts either a particular piece of or narrates a summary of God's story of divine presence with a particular focus on the end of the story.

But the sermon takes God's gracious activity of salvation for us in Jesus Christ, proclaimed in all these pieces, and joins it uniquely to the life of the saint who died in the faith. It declares that the death of every one of God's saints, including this one, is precious to Him (see Ps 116:15). And it is for this moment, for this reason, that Jesus laid down His life only to take it back up again. He was delivered up to death so that we may not die eternally.[94] And "because He is now risen from the dead and lives and reigns to all eternity," every believer in Christ, especially this believer, "will overcome sin and death and will rise again to new life."[95] It comforts Christians who mourn with the reality that death is not the end of our story.

Having heard the certainty of the resurrection to eternal life that is ours in Christ Jesus our Lord, we, God's people, longingly cast all our cares upon Christ, knowing that He will sustain us as we await the glorious day of His coming. We pray that the Church be given Christ's light and peace, daily die to sin and rise to the newness of life, be raised to immortality and incorruption, and pass with Christ through the gate of death and the grave to our joyful resurrection.[96] We pray that the family of the saint who died and all who mourn receive the comfort and consolation of Jesus' love and find courage, faith, and strength in the weekly Divine Service as they patiently wait for eternal life with Jesus, along with their loved one who

---

94 *LSB*, p. 263.
95 *LSB*, p. 208.
96 *LSB Agenda*, p. 121.

died in the faith.[97] Finally, we give thanks that Jesus's death has destroyed the power of death, His resurrection has opened the kingdom of heaven to all believers, and there is now nothing that can separate us from the love of God in Christ Jesus.[98]

Since Christ is present with us in His word, we do not have to wait for or wonder about His response to our petitions and thanksgiving. Jesus swiftly and emphatically answers "Yes!" Actually, His words are more poignant than that: "'I am the resurrection and the life,' says the Lord. 'He who believes in Me will live, even though he dies; and whoever lives and believes in Me will never die.'"[99] These words make us fervently yearn to depart from this vale of tears, this valley of sorrows, and be with Christ. That is why our response to the voice of our Good Shepherd is to sing with Simeon the Nunc Dimittis, asking the Lord to let us depart in peace.[100]

He does. Jesus gives us His mercy, grace, presence, and peace in the familiar words of the Aaronic benediction: "The Lord bless you and keep you. The Lord make His face shine upon you and be gracious unto you. The Lord lift up His countenance upon you and give you peace."[101] And as we depart to the cemetery with the casket of our beloved saint in hand, we do not go in silence but with singing. For death cannot silence the voice of Jesus, nor does it get the final word. Death cannot end our gladness.[102]

Even as we walk toward the grave at the cemetery and watch the pall-bearers place the casket on the lowering device, the voice of Jesus shatters the silence of death. The comforting Word of Christ rings out in psalms and hymns spoken and sung by God's chosen instrument, your pastor. "I [Jesus] am the resurrection and the life. I know my Redeemer lives. And after my skin has been destroyed, this I know, that in my flesh I shall see God. You will not abandon my soul to Sheol. I shall not die, but I shall live."[103] Christ's words remind us of what our eyes cannot see but what our ears hear and our hearts long for: the victory of eternal life in Christ

---

97 *LSB Agenda*, p. 121.

98 *LSB Agenda*, p. 121.

99 *LSB*, p. 281.

100 *LSB*, p. 281.

101 *LSB*, p. 281.

102 See *LSB* 594.

103 These passages are my synthesis of Jn 11:25; Jb 19:25–26; Ps 16:10; 118:17 taken from the start of the Committal service in *Lutheran Service Book: Pastoral Care Companion* (St. Louis: Concordia Publishing House, 2007), 125–30.

Jesus our Lord.

As Jesus' body and grave were reverently, deliberately, and lovingly prepared by His saints, so are ours. First, the pastor asks Jesus, who hallowed or made holy the graves of all believers through His three-day rest in the tomb, to bless this grave so that the body of His beloved believer may quietly rest in it until the day of the resurrection of all flesh.[104] Jesus' blessing of the grave turns our fierce foe into a calm companion. What once sought to swallow and consume our bodies whole now serves as a narrow chamber for peaceful sleep.[105]

Second, the pastor uses dirt from the freshly dug grave to make the sign of the cross on top of the casket. The dirt vividly declares the curse of the First Adam, the wages of sin. Our bodies, which were created by God from the dust of the ground, will return to the dust of the ground (see Gn 3:19). But the shape of the cross brilliantly proclaims the glory of the Second Adam, Jesus Christ our Lord, "who will change our lowly bodies so that they will be like His glorious body, by the power that enables Him to subdue all things to Himself."[106]

In the meantime, God the Father, who created our bodies, God the Son, who redeemed our bodies by His blood, and God the Holy Spirit, who made our bodies His temple, will guard and keep them as He has promised.[107] He will continue to abide with us in death, as He has throughout our earthly lives. He will allow our bodies to rest in peace and joy until Christ returns and awakens them to eternal life.

So that we may more confidently believe in the resurrection of the body and the life everlasting in the face of our great and powerful enemy death, one final triumphant Easter battle cry arises from the graveside: "Alleluia! Christ is risen! He is risen indeed. Alleluia!"[108] These words impart a lasting strength, hope, mercy, and comfort that the world does not know and cannot give. Everything else in this world will perish. All our possessions, fame, fortune, health, family, and friends will be stripped away from us by death. Even so, death has not won. The seal of the grave is forever broken. We go into the grave only to inevitably follow Christ out of the

---

104 *LSB Pastoral Care Companion*, p. 131.
105 See *LSB* 708.
106 *LSB Pastoral Care Companion*, p. 134.
107 *LSB Pastoral Care Companion*, p. 134.
108 *LSB Pastoral Care Companion*, p. 135.

grave. For everyone who looks on the Son, everyone who believes in Jesus, has eternal life, and He will raise them up on the Last Day (see Jn 6:40).

"When will that day occur? And what will it be like?" you might wonder. You are not alone. Throughout history, many people have asked the same questions concerning the Last Day. Some have even tried, and I suspect will continue trying, to calculate the exact day it will occur. But the truth is you can't calculate the date and time of the Last Day, the Day of the Resurrection of all flesh when Christ returns in all His glory. Nor should you try. Sure, you can see the condition of the world worsening. You can see hatred, betrayal, wars, rumors of wars, famines, earthquakes, false prophets, lawlessness, and martyrdom, and rightly believe, like Peter (see 1Pt 4:7), Martin Luther,[109] and countless others, that the end is near (see Mt 24:3–13). However, these are only signs, initial birth pains, the beginning of the end. Jesus told His disciples that no one knows the precise day or the hour, not the angels nor the Son, but only the Father (see Mt 24:36). The Father has appointed the time, and it is not ours to know (see Ac 1:7).

What we do know is that the Last Day will come suddenly and unexpectedly, like a thief in the night (see 1Th 5:2). What happened in Noah's day before the great flood will also occur on the Last Day (see Lk 17:26–27). People will go about their regular, day-to-day activities of eating, drinking, sleeping, working, buying, selling, and even starting families. Then, at an hour that we do not expect, Jesus will return (see Mt 24:44). As previously stated, He will "descend from heaven with a cry of command, with the voice of an archangel, and with the sound of the trumpet of God" (1Th 4:16). Every last person who has died, beginning with Adam at the beginning up to that Final Day, will hear Jesus' voice and come out of the grave (see Jn 5:25, 28–29; 1Co 15:22). Their bodies and souls shall be reunited. And the dead who were raised, together with those who are still alive at Christ's coming, will all "meet the Lord in the air" (1Th 4:17) and appear before His judgment seat (see 2Co 5:10).

A great separation will occur when Jesus judges both the living and the dead. He will separate believers from unbelievers (see Mt 13:36–42) "as a shepherd separates the sheep from the goats" (Mt 25:32). Those who have heard and believed God's message of salvation for them in Jesus

---

109 In AE 50:245, Luther writes, "It looks to me as if the world, too, has come to the hour of its passing, and has become an old worn out coat (as the Psalm says), which soon has to be changed."

Christ proclaimed by His chosen instruments will be placed on Jesus' right. Those who have heard and ignored or rejected God's message of salvation for them in Jesus Christ proclaimed by His chosen instruments will be placed on Jesus' left. Then the great separation will occur. The believers on the right will receive the judgment of eternal life and shall enter heaven, while the unbelievers on the left will receive the judgment of eternal condemnation and shall enter hell (see Jn 5:29; Dn 12:2).

Often, when we think of heaven and hell, we tend to think about them like we do the Divine Service, with respect to ourselves. Hence you often hear many Christians speak of heaven in terms of what they love to do and the things that bring them joy here on earth. So, if I like to sing, I get to sing in the heavenly choir. If I like to play basketball, football, baseball, soccer, hockey, or some other sport, I get to play on the Lord's team. If I like to garden or farm, I will be tending the Lord's garden or fields. If I love people, then I will be enjoying a grand reunion, catching up with, laughing, and enjoying the company of everyone I love in this life. Hell is likewise described in self-centered terms. I can't even tell you the number of times I have heard people say, "Well, if I'm going to hell, at least I will be there with my friends and family."

Yet again, we should not think of ourselves more highly than we ought (see Rm 12:3). Just as God's story is not centered in or around you or me, neither is heaven or hell. To be sure, when Scripture speaks of heaven, it depicts immense joy. When it speaks of hell, incomprehensible misery. But the reason for the joy or misery is not you. It is the unveiled presence of the living God.

"Depart from Me," Jesus will say to the unbelievers on His left (Mt 25:41). At His word of judgment, they shall depart from Christ and His holy angels into the eternal fire (see Rv 14:10). A great chasm will be forever fixed between Him and them (see Lk 16:26). Those who ignored or rejected God's message of salvation here in time will enter into the place that was "prepared for the devil and his angels" (Mt 25:41) and suffer God's wrath, that is eternal punishment and torment "away from the presence of the Lord and from the glory of His might" (2Th 1:9). They who once received God's good gifts of food, clothes, family, love, protection, and care through His varied masks, or people, will do so no longer. Unbelievers will be permanently away from the presence of Jesus, the true light of the world (see Jn 8:12), the giver of living water (see Jn 4:10; 7:37–39), and the very kindness and love of God (see Ti 3:4). Consequently, they will perpetually experience darkness (see Mt 8:12), unquenchable fire (see Mk 9:48), insatiable thirst (see Lk 16:24), and unbearable physical, mental, and emotional anguish (see Lk 16:25). "In that place there will be weeping and gnashing of teeth" (Mt 25:30).

But to those on Jesus' right, to you and all the believers who are clothed in their wedding garments, which are the baptismal robe of Christ's righteousness, He will say, "Come, you who are blessed by my Father, inherit the kingdom prepared for you from the foundation of the world" (Mt 25:34). At His word of judgment, Jesus will take us to be with Him in that heavenly Jerusalem, Mount Zion. On that mountain, all that we have been watching, waiting, and longing for since the days of the first Adam will be brought to completion and fully restored. The Lord of Sabaoth, the general of the heavenly armies, Jesus Himself, will permanently crush the head of the serpent, Satan, under His and our feet (see 1Co 15:25; Rm 16:20). He will completely deliver us from the bondage of sin by eternally removing it from us (see 1Jn 3:2; Rv 7:14). He will destroy and swallow up death forever (see Is 25:8; 1Co 15:26, 54–55). He will make all things new (see Rv 21:5). And at long last, "the dwelling place of God is [now] with man. He will dwell with them, and they will be His people, and God Himself will be with them as their God" (Rv 21:3). The presence of God, which was veiled and which we enjoyed in the Divine Service for one hour a week here in time, will now be unveiled and enjoyed for all eternity. And with our own newly resurrected, immortal, sin-free eyes, we will see God face-to-face (see Jb 19:27; Rv 22:4).

When we live with and under the one true God—Father, Son, and Holy Spirit—in His kingdom, we will not need the sun, moon, or stars. The glory of God and the Lamb will be our light (see Rv 21:23). We will not hunger or thirst. At the marriage feast of the Lamb, we will eat from the tree of life (see Rv 2:7), feast on rich food and well-aged wine (see Is 25:6), and be guided to springs of living water (see Rv 7:17). There will be no mourning, crying, or pain anymore (see Rv 21:4), because God will shelter us with His presence (see Rv 7:15). He will wipe every last tear from our eyes (Is 25:8; Rv 7:17; 21:4). We will want for and lack nothing. For in God's presence, at His right hand, there is peace, fullness of joy, and pleasures forevermore (see Ps 16:11).

Can you even imagine what it will be like to no longer wonder, "Where is the Promised Child who will crush the head of the serpent and restore to us the presence of God?" or, "Where is the Promised Child who has crushed the head of the serpent, and when will He return to restore to us the unveiled presence of God?" but to eternally rejoice that Jesus, the Promised Child, has permanently crushed the head of the serpent and eternally restored us to the presence of God? Can you see yourself standing around the throne of God with Adam, Abraham, Isaac, Jacob, Moses, Elijah, Isaiah, Jeremiah, Ezekiel, Mary Magdalene, Peter, John, Mary the mother of Jesus, and all the faithful and countless Christians throughout the ages triumphantly waving your palm branch and crying out, "Salvation belongs to our God who sits on the throne, and to the Lamb" (Rv 7:10)? Can you picture yourself living in, with, and under Christ at the end of God's breathtakingly beautiful story? It is nearer now than when you first picked up this book.

But whether you are here in time or there in eternity, one thing is certain. Your life, dear Christian, is firmly rooted and intricately woven into the unified biblical narrative of God's presence in the person and work of Jesus Christ, into whom you were incorporated by Baptism, with whom you abide each week in the Divine Service, and under whom you and all believers will live at the resurrection. More simply stated, your life is and always will be lived in Christ.

APPENDIX: UNITY OF CONFESSION

When you step up to the altar to receive Holy Communion, you are not alone. You come forward with your fellow Christians who have gathered with you in a particular church building, located in a particular area, at a particular time, for a particular purpose. Together, as the Body of Christ, you all come forward so that you may intimately dwell in God's presence and receive the forgiveness of sins as you eat and drink the very body and blood of our Lord Jesus Christ in, with, and under the bread and wine. Sadly, not everyone always receives the same benefit.

Hold on. What I fear you heard me just say was, "When Christians step up to the altar, they do not all receive the same thing." But what I said was, "Not everyone always receives the same benefit." There is a big difference.

If I use the word *thing*, my focus tends to be more on the *object* that I eat and drink in the Lord's Supper. Consequently, the object is called into question. But the object is not in question. You don't have to wonder, "Is this really Jesus' body and blood sacramentally united to the bread and wine, or is it bread and wine that represent the body and blood of Jesus?" On the night of Jesus' betrayal, He took bread. About that bread, He said, "Take, eat; this is My body" (Mt 26:26). Similarly, He took the cup of wine and said, "Drink of it, all of you, for this is My blood of the covenant, which is poured out for many for the forgiveness of sins" (Mt 26:27–28). Moreover, the apostle Paul confirmed this when he said this to the saints in Corinth:

> I received from the Lord what I also delivered to you, that the Lord Jesus on the night when He was betrayed took bread, and when He had given thanks, He broke it, and said, "This is My body, which is for you. Do this in remembrance of Me." In the same way also He took the cup, after supper, saying, "This cup is the new covenant in My blood. Do this, as often as you drink it, in remembrance of Me." (1Co 11:23–25)

Subsequently, everyone who comes to the altar and participates in the Lord's Supper by eating the bread and wine also receives the body and blood of Jesus. They receive bread, which is the body of Christ, and wine, which is the blood of Christ, not because they believe it but because it is Jesus' word.

If it helps, let me give you an analogy. Suppose you and I wish to go skydiving. We board a plane, ascend to an altitude of 10,560 feet, or 2 miles, and begin to approach the drop zone. Before we jump, there is one thing you need to know. You may well believe that gravity exists and thus have a parachute strapped on your back. I, however, do not believe in gravity, so I do not have a parachute. When we jump, what will happen? Will you fall to the ground at 9.807 meters per second squared because you believe gravity exists, while I hover in the air because I do not believe in gravity's existence? Does my faith determine gravity's existence? No. Gravity is an absolute. It exists whether I believe it or not. Both of us will fall at 9.807 meters per second squared. Similarly, your faith does not determine whether Christ's body and blood are present in, with, and under the bread and wine or not. He who said to the wind and the waves, "Be still" (Mk 4:39), and they obeyed, says about the bread and wine, "This is My body; this is My blood," and so they are.

However, even though everyone who participates in the Lord's Supper receives the same object or thing—bread, which is the body of Christ, and wine, which is the blood of Christ—not everyone always receives the same benefit or intended outcome. In skydiving, the intended benefit is exhilarating fun and the enjoyment of creation from a bird's-eye view as you float safely to the ground. In the Lord's Supper, the intended benefit of eating and drinking Christ's body and blood is "the forgiveness of sins" (Mt 26:28). Yet it is possible to go skydiving and receive the exact opposite of a safe, exhilarating, and breathtakingly beautiful time. It is possible to jump and die. Similarly, it is possible to eat and drink the body and blood of Christ in the Lord's Supper and receive the exact opposite of the forgiveness of sins. In short, it is possible to receive the Lord's Supper and incur God's judgment and wrath (see 1Co 11:27, 29).

This is what was happening at the Church in Corinth. There were many who were coming to Holy Communion, but instead of receiving the forgiveness of sins, they received God's judgment. Many became weak and ill, and a few even died (see 1Co 11:30). Why? Because the church was divided (see 1Co 11:18). Several Christians had exchanged the wisdom of God, the very mind of Christ, for the wisdom of man (see 1Co 1:10–3:21). They had departed from the truth, meaning Christ and His Word, on several issues. Instead of believing the truth and confessing Him with their mouths and lives or conduct, they had begun believing and living in ways that were contrary to Him. Concerning the matter of the Lord's Supper, they were eating and drinking in an unworthy manner, without discerning the body of Christ (see 1Co 11:29).

When you hear the phrase "discerning the body of Christ," you might think that the Corinthian Christians' issue was that many people thought the bread and wine were not actually Jesus' body and blood but merely represented them. It was not. The "is" versus "represents" controversy was not prominent until the Sacramentarians of the 1500s during the Reformation.[110] Before that time, the Church predominantly regarded Holy Communion as the body and blood of Christ sacramentally united to the external elements of bread and wine by the power of Christ's Word.[111] The Corinthian Christians' issue was that they were treating the Lord's Supper and their fellow Christians like they were nothing. When they came together for a communal meal, which incorporated the celebration of the Lord's Supper, some of the wealthier church members grew impatient and ate everything before the day laborers and slaves could arrive.[112] Hence, St. Paul says, "One goes ahead with his own meal. One goes hungry, another gets drunk" (1Co 11:21). Their words and actions demonstrated that there was a division between God and their fellow man.

Jesus had said, "Take, eat; this is My body . . . this is My blood" (Mt 26:26–28), but the Corinthian Christians were treating Holy Communion as if it were just an ordinary meal. They acted like Jesus, the Lord most holy, wasn't present and as if they weren't feasting on His body and blood. Similarly, He had said, "A new commandment I give to you, that you love one another: just as I have loved you, you also are to love one another" (Jn 13:34). But they were despising their fellow Christians, the Body of Christ, and humiliating them, thus causing great harm (see 1Co 11:17, 22). What's more, they didn't even seem to care that they had rejected Jesus' Word and were hating their fellow brothers in Christ. How do we know? Because they just kept doing it. Celebration after celebration, they kept

---

110 FC SD VII

111 For an in-depth discussion and analysis of the Early Church's understanding of Holy Communion pre-Middle Ages, see Martin Chemnitz, *The Lord's Supper: De coena Domini,* trans. J.A.O. Preus (St. Louis: Concordia Publishing House, 1979), 149–83.

112 Gregory J. Lockwood, *1 Corinthians,* Concordia Commentary (St. Louis: Concordia Publishing House, 2000), 384.

bringing the divisions between themselves before the Lord and acting like the divisions did not exist. They acted like they believed God's Word and were living according to it when they weren't. In so doing, they were essentially lying to God. And "lying lips are an abomination to the Lord, but those who act faithfully are His delight" (Pr 12:22). Thus they received God's judgment instead of His forgiveness, as many became weak and ill, and a few even died (see 1Co 11:30).

So that they might repent of their sin, believe Christ's true Word once again, be reconciled to God and one another, and receive Holy Communion together in unity, Paul admonished them using the very thing that was given to him: the Word of Christ. Paul reiterated Jesus' words about how the bread is Jesus' body and the wine is Jesus' blood (see 1Co 11:23–25). Having reconciled their divisions between God and their fellow saints, he further instructed them to examine or judge themselves using the measure of God's Holy Word, which he had just spoken to them (see 1Co 11:27, 31). In doing so, they would be able to discern the body. That is, they would be able to determine whether their beliefs and actions concerning eating and drinking the body and blood of Jesus with the Body of Christ, their fellow Christians, were in accordance with God's Word. By confirming this unity of confession through examination, the Body of Christ could confidently participate as one unified body in the Lord's Supper and receive the benefit of the forgiveness of sins.

Paul's words to the Christians in Corinth are no less authoritative and applicable for us today. Even now, we are responsible for examining our beliefs and actions before we come forward with our fellow members of the Body of Christ to eat and drink the body/bread and blood/wine of Christ in the Lord's Supper.[113] We are to ensure that what we believe and how we live, both personally and publicly, are in agreement with God's Word so that there will be no divisions among us when we stand before God (see 1Co 1:10). That is why Jesus says, "If you are offering your gift at the altar and there remember that your brother has something against you, leave your gift there before the altar and go. First be reconciled to your brother" (Mt 5:23–24). We are never to bring our divisions before the Lord and act like they don't exist or don't matter. We are never to

---

113 A list of questions for self-examination before receiving the Sacrament of the Altar can be found in *LSB*, pp. 329–30.

come to the Lord's Table and act like there are no divisions if there are. To do that is to lie to God and thus sin against the Body of Christ, as well as the body and blood of Christ.

When a personal or public sin that causes division between God and our fellow man is identified or pointed out (see Mt 18:15–17), such as false doctrines or teachings, evil thoughts, murder, adultery, coveting, sexual immorality, sensuality, deceit, theft, false witness, slander, envy, pride, holding grudges, and many others, we must reconcile. We must repent of our sins, confess that sin before God and one another, receive forgiveness, and bear the fruit of repentance by turning from our erroneous beliefs and sinful ways. When reconciliation occurs, unity of the body is restored. And "how good and pleasant it is when brothers dwell in unity" (Ps 133:1). So good and pleasant that we, like the Christians in Corinth, may in faith and unity of confession come to the Lord's Table and confidently participate as one unified body in His Holy Supper, receiving the benefits of the forgiveness of our sins, strengthening of our faith, and an intimate fellowship with Christ and one another.

BIBLIOGRAPHY

American Bible Society. "State of the Bible 2017." https://1s712.americanbible. org/state-of-the-bible/stateofthebible/State_of_the_bible-2017.pdf (accessed July 29, 2022).

———"State of the Bible 2022." https://1s712.americanbible.org/state-of-the-bible/ stateofthebible/State_of_the_bible-2022.pdf (accessed July 29, 2022).

Chemnitz, Martin. *Ministry, Word, and Sacraments: An Enchiridion*. Translated by Luther Poellot. St. Louis: Concordia Publishing House, 1981.

———*The Lord's Supper: De coena Domini*. Translated by J.A.O. Preus. St. Louis: Concordia Publishing House, 1979.

Commission on Worship of The Lutheran Church—Missouri Synod. *Lutheran Service Book: Agenda*. St. Louis: Concordia Publishing House, 2006.

———*Lutheran Service Book: Altar Book*. St. Louis: Concordia Publishing House, 2006.

———*Lutheran Service Book: Pew Edition*. St. Louis: Concordia Publishing House, 2006.

———*Lutheran Service Book: Pastoral Care Companion*. St. Louis: Concordia Publishing House, 2007.

The Holy Bible. *English Standard Version*. Wheaton, IL: Crossway, 2016.

Just, Arthur A. *Heaven on Earth: The Gifts of Christ in the Divine Service*. St. Louis: Concordia Publishing House, 2008.

Korcok, Thomas. *Lutheran Education: From Wittenberg to the Future*. St. Louis: Concordia Publishing House, 2011.

Lessing, R. Reed, and Andrew E. Steinmann. *Prepare the Way of the Lord: An Introduction to the Old Testament*. St. Louis: Concordia Publishing House, 2014.

Lockwood, Gregory J. *1 Corinthians*, Concordia Commentary, St. Louis: Concordia Publishing House. 2000.

Luther, Martin. *Luther's Works*, volume 1, *Lectures on Genesis: Chapters 1–5*. Edited by J. J. Pelikan, H. C. Oswald, and H. T. Lehmann. St. Louis: Concordia Publishing House, 1999.

———*Luther's Works*, volume 9, *Lectures on Deuteronomy*. Edited by J. J. Pelikan, H. C. Oswald, and H. T. Lehmann, Eds. St. Louis: Concordia Publishing House, 1999.

———*Luther's Works*, volume 14, *Selected Psalms III*. Edited by J. J. Pelikan, H. C. Oswald, & H. T. Lehmann. St. Louis: Concordia Publishing House, 1999.

———*Luther's Works*, volume 50, *Letters III*. Edited by J. J. Pelikan, H. C. Oswald, & H. T. Lehmann. St. Louis: Concordia Publishing House, 1999.

Maxwell, Lee A. *The Altar Guild Manual: Lutheran Service Book Edition*. St. Louis: Concordia Publishing House, 2008.

Concordia: The Lutheran Confessions, second edition, St. Louis: Concordia Publishing House, 2006.

Orthodox Church in America. "Paschal Troparion." Accessed May 28, 2022. https://www.oca.org/orthodoxy/prayers/selected-liturgical-hymns.

Precht, Fred L. *Lutheran Worship: History and Practice*. St. Louis: Concordia Publishing House, 1993.

Steinmann, Andrew E. *From Abraham to Paul*. St. Louis: Concordia Publishing House, 2011.